Crossing the Borderline

Journaling a Journey from Madness and Mayhem to Faith and Forgiveness.

T. R. Lilly

ISBN 978-1-64028-797-6 (paperback)
ISBN 978-1-64028-798-3 (digital)

Copyright © 2017 by T. R. Lilly

All rights reserved. No part of this publication may be reproduced, distributed, or transmitted in any form or by any means, including photocopying, recording, or other electronic or mechanical methods without the prior written permission of the publisher. For permission requests, solicit the publisher via the address below.

Christian Faith Publishing
832 Park Avenue
Meadville, PA 16335
www.christianfaithpublishing.com

For more information on Crossing the Borderline or T. R. Lilly, visit www.trlilly.com.

Printed in the United States of America

Contents

Preface 5

1: The Backstory 9

2: Back to Work 15

3: Walking through the Therapist Door Again Years Later 19

4: Borderline Personality Disorder (BPD) 23

5: Bipolar 27

5.5: Bipolar—Here Is What I Should Have Written 34

6: What's in Your Backpack? 37

7: Why Bother? And How It All Starts 40

8: You've Got a Decision to Make 44

9: Shifting the Perception of Normal 46

10: Medication Stigmata 49

11: It's Not Really about My Story 57

12: Admitting It Is Half the Battle 60

13: Okay, So Half the Battle May Have Been Overstating Things a Bit 63

14: I'm Not Ready Yet 68

15: I Don't Want to Do This Anymore 72

16: The Games I've Played 76

17: Why Me? 78

18: What's Fair? (I think It's that Thing that Happens on the County Fairground Once a Year with the Good Food and the Parade)..81

19: It Really Is as Scary as It Looks (aka Do Try This at Home)...86

20: The Madness Within..91

21: Leaving the Past in the Past (The PTSD Chapter).................95

22: Oh, Be Careful, Little Mouth, What You Say........................98

23: The Double Bind 103

24: Programmed Responses...107

25: Be Busy Being You 110

26: Adrenaline Crush 112

27: Who Moved Last? 115

28: The Last Time Was the Last Time, Right? 120

29: Sleep Deprivation..123

30: It Hurts the Most When There Is Pain 128

31: Alone in the Desert 130

32: One Favorite Thing...135

33: Everything Looks So Much Easier from the Outside 138

34: The Cut Is Shallow, but the Pain Runs Deep.......................142

35: Measuring Up 144

36: I'm Not So Different After All...146

Epilogue...149

Preface

So I was sitting in church one Wednesday night, and the person teaching the class actually made this statement: "It's not like I'm writing a book about all of my shortcomings and faults. Who would do that!" It was said at a time when this book was just beginning to be written. There is no good answer to that question, but in a lot of ways, that is exactly what this book is.

This book is as much about my own misconceptions as it is about the truth. It is about the stigma of being diagnosed with a mental illness I didn't have and being given the correct diagnosis of a disorder that had affected my life for years without my even knowing it. I didn't have a good answer to the question that was asked that night, but I already knew that this is what this book would become.

Crossing the Borderline has as much to do with feeling like you have to hide everything from everyone as it does the games we play with those we love and those who are trying to help us. This book is not just about feeling broken or like a freak or a monster, but also about being someone who is, in fact, broken and afraid that he or she will infect all the "nice, normal, happy" people.

It's about walking away from God and coming home to find out that you never really understood who God was in the first place. It's about growing up in a normal family and feeling like (or being) the black sheep and an outcast—not having anyone understand that you are just trying to help them and, at the same time, not knowing how or being able to help yourself.

Crossing the Borderline is about my shortcomings, mistakes, errors, faults, depression, and desperation. It is about doing more than just figuring out that I need help and finally finding the right places to get it after spending a good bit of time in a lot of the wrong ones. It's getting lost in the wrong diagnosis and then manipulating everyone and everything because I was sure it was the right thing to do for everyone's sake and then actually committing to the process and knowing that I have to honestly show up every single day for it even if I didn't have therapy scheduled for that day. It's also about taking the meds I need and acknowledging that they work, so I need to keep taking them.

So back to the original question. Why write this book? First, I have to admit that this didn't start out as a book. It started out as a few journal entries that I shared with some friends who said they thought people need to read to hear the truth. Well, the true answer to this question actually is a rather simple one. There are so many of us out there. We are the broken and the hurting. The misdiagnosed, correctly diagnosed, not diagnosed at all, or incorrectly diagnosed with mental illness when we are just trying to cope with life as we know it despite not wanting to carry a diagnosis at all. We are afraid to get help because it will make us look like a freak or crazy or untouchable.

This book is a chance for us to identify. You may not identify with me or the situations that I've been in. You may identify with one of my caregivers or friends. You may think of me as someone you know or someone who is like you or—who knows—maybe even someone you hope you will never meet. The thing is that everything we have done until the point in which I am writing this (and you are reading it) is part of who we are. So the faults in this book are a part of me. Transparently, many of them are parts of my past that I'm not proud of or don't like very much. They are all, however, lessons learned, and they all continue to lead me to the place where I finally walked through the door, looking for real help in trying to figure out how I'm supposed to do more than just live life because we were all meant to thrive!

I'm hoping this book will help remove people from the stereotypes and make us all seem a bit more "normal." One of the realities of life is that we all start out at the same spot in the journey, and we will all come to the same point in the end. The difference is the journey we take, that first step, and the time we spend figuring out how to live our lives and deciding if we are going to be crossing the borderline.

1

The Backstory

Everything starts with the backstory. The thing is, mine isn't all that different from hundreds of thousands of others that are out there, and it turns out it's not about the backstory at all. It turns out that the story really begins with these words I'm about to hear. So over a decade ago, I was sitting in this chair in this cold clinical office, waiting to hear what was wrong with me, why I had all the *craziness* going on in my brain or, for that matter, my life. It didn't even matter in this moment that I was just discharged a few days ago from what would prove to be the first of several inpatient admissions to a locked psych unit.

It doesn't matter who you are. I firmly believe that everyone thinks it will never be them. Sitting here, waiting to hear what brand of crazy (mental illness) I'd been labeled with, it didn't even really occur (in the moment) that this was really happening and that this was my life. It turned out that in the moment, sitting in this chair was the one thing that I had not made up, twisted, or made bigger than what it was. This was that actual next step to the rest of the journey.

Sitting here, waiting for the psychiatrist to sit down and get started, I remember hearing the door latch for that first time a couple of weeks ago—the door to a locked psych unit. They called it voluntary commitment, but for me, that was the last thing I wanted to do. In my case, it came down to me making the decision to commit myself or my family doc making that decision for me. I use the term *voluntary* loosely because agreeing to be locked in an inpatient adult mental health unit of a hospital meant that what I would rather do was just jump off the planet. The thing nobody knew, and the only thing I knew for sure as that closing door echoed down that long hallway, was that I was not right. When it came to what I knew, I was just an overly emotional disappointment. I was a chick who made bad decisions who had blown every good relationship she had ever had, who needed to control every bad thing that could happen, and who would never be anything in life. What I didn't know and what I tried to hide was that I was a liar, slick as ice, manipulative, erratic, impulsive, and scared to my socks that I'd never be fixed or ever become anything.

Sitting in this chair now with that admission behind me, what I thought I knew was that I'd done my best until this point in my life and still messed up every single thing I'd touched. As a matter of fact, I had figured out that I was responsible for a lot of things I couldn't even control. I was responsible for the happiness of others or lack thereof. I had to throw myself on metaphorical and figurative landmines that hadn't even exploded yet or might not exist. I had to see trip wires that were invisible in relationships and defuse the bombs before they go off.

The killer thing, and I didn't realize this as I was sitting in the chair, waiting for my diagnoses, was that I didn't even know what a healthy relationship was or looked like because I'd never let anyone get close to me. I'd been hurt physically, emotionally, sexually, and I didn't know how to have a real relationship of any kind with anyone I came in contact with.

Yet here I sat, waiting to hear what was wrong with me. You can call it a label or a diagnosis. At the time, it felt like a sentence (just like prison); either way, here it came.

At this point (the moment in which I sat in the chair), none of this was familiar language to me. He started out with the primary diagnosis: bipolar (manic depression) and, secondarily, borderline personality disorder. What? I didn't use these terms every day.

Actually, I'm not sure that I'd much more than heard of bipolar, and I didn't know anything about this borderline thing. So now, I was scared and I was alone in this and I was in for the fight of my life because whatever was wrong with me, there was no way it could be what he just said.

I just got out of the locked inpatient unit where I was diagnosed as being depressed, and now, my entire self-image had changed. How was I supposed to move forward? Depression to someone "like me"—to someone who wanted to exit life just for a single moment or intermittently, someone who has no background in psychology or sociology—was a word that was catch-all, taking in everyone from someone who is having a bad day or can't cope with a bad grade or winter.

In terms that are probably a little bit inaccurate but were easy for me to understand, the bipolar thing meant that my life was a roller coaster. It explained the highs and lows and that they were cyclical; for me, the cycle was rapid. But there are different types of bipolar, and they are numbered. And this diagnosis did answer a few questions for me like the inability to sleep and having crazy periods of energy.

The borderline personality disorder (moving forward, I will refer to it as BPD) is this thing that I had never even heard of before. All I knew was it didn't sound good and that it made me sound like some kind of social monster (which kind of matched how I felt). As I sat in that chair, in that moment, I just knew that I was broken, and I had no idea of the journey that lay ahead of me.

This psychiatrist (med doc) had been talking for at least ten or twenty minutes now, and I hadn't really heard a word since he named the diagnoses. I'm surprised to find that my own voice was shaking as I asked, "What is bipolar?" Until he told me this diagnosis, I didn't even think I needed to be here. I was well enough to be released from the unit. The only reason I even set up the appointment was because it was on the list of things you have to do to be released and get them to unlock the door and let you walk back outside.

In all fairness to the account I'm giving you, you should try to understand that this is just one side of the story. I was still numb or in shock as he answered my questions, so this may not be the most accurate representation of the facts but it is the absolute truth as I remember it. What I heard him say was that this (bipolar) is an illness that is spawned from a chemical imbalance in the brain. It causes a person to go back and forth between states of depression and euphoria or mania. It is something that can be treated with a combination of medications (some of which require monitoring of level through blood work) and talk therapy.

Okay, and the borderline thing? I had it "so together" I couldn't even remember what it was called. Borderline personality disorder was a totally different story. The definition I remember from that day wasn't really a definition at all. I just knew when I left the office that day that I was certain that both diagnoses were right. It was evident by my mood and by my actions and reactions. There was even more proof in how I handled relationships—or didn't handle them might be a better way to describe it. There were meds to help with the bipolar thing but the borderline personality disorder was more of a wild card, and there wasn't a specific med or list of medicine options for that one. However, this was the reason that I had such unstable relationships, and there wasn't a med that could help me with this one. *Great News!*

During this entire appointment, all I was trying to figure out was where to go from here. I was in my mid-twenties, just a few years into a marriage that was coming unglued at the seams and, as it turns out, on a long road that turned out to be one bad path after another. I would love to sit here and tell you I didn't know better, and on some fronts that is the absolute truth. I grew up with a family that loved me. I knew and talked to all my grandparents, aunts, uncles and cousins. We did the family vacation thing every year even after I married (my parents made sure I was able to go if at all possible). When I was a child, my parents, my sister, and myself went to church as often the doors were open.

CROSSING THE BORDERLINE

I grew up in two great places—a town in West Virginia that I still call home and a place in Pennsylvania that's home too.

Even with all that—a diagnosis of bipolar and BPD from a psychiatrist (which is a med doc as opposed to a psychologist, which is a therapist with no scriptwriting ability)—the two paragraphs above this one was the story I told myself for years. Kind of the abbreviated version of my life up until I was twenty-six. It was all true … every word. There was a lot that was left out of it too, but that didn't matter to me because a doctor had now redefined who I am.

Did I mention that I am also the daughter of a registered nurse? So as the kid of a medical professional, I learned to trust doctors and their staff, which isn't such a bad thing if you are capable of being your own advocate. That day, as I sat in that chair, I wasn't equipped to do that. In the years to come, someone would say take this pill, and I would. You need a blood draw, so I jumped off that bridge too. After all, they went through school and got the big diploma, so I'm sure they know what they're doing … right?

There is a long time—years between that moment in the chair and the time that I'm fast-forwarding too. There are these amazing friends that I "lucked" into. Luck is just another word for God helping me without me knowing it at the time. A man and his wife and, in time, their son. They were there for me in ways that I can't begin to explain.

I spent years being medicated for a condition I didn't have. What the psychiatrist thought was bipolar turned out to be low self-esteem. The BPD diagnosis was correct. The thing is these friends of mine encouraged me and loved me and prayed for me. Many were the nights when I cried at their kitchen table because I didn't know what to do. I remember my friend's husband, a man of God and an auto mechanic, telling me that I didn't need the meds, and they were doing more harm than good. How that man who had nothing close to a medical degree was able to figure that out what was going on when the rest of the world couldn't is beyond me.

I thank God that throughout my life, he has surrounded me with people who know more and have more life experience than I do. Right now, I'm on two psych meds—one for depression and one for anxiety (we'll get into that more later), and I have one I take for sleep as needed.

Meds can definitely be a part of the equation, but for me, it turned out to not be what I needed the most as I tried to figure out how to cross the borderline.

2

Back to Work

When you're talking about addiction, they call it rock bottom. You know, that place where you've come to the end of the road and you know you're going to need help if you're going to recover. I'm not aware of any kind of specific psych term for it when we are talking about mental or emotional instability, but it's pretty much the same thing. It's that day when you wake up and start paying enough attention to look around and see things for what they are. A mess!

For me, it really didn't happen totally until I made some changes in my life. It was years after I found out I was misdiagnosed and after I stopped using the locked inpatient unit as a getaway to hide out and get things back together enough to be able to

1. Contract for my own safety
2. Get back to living what is considered a high functioning life
3. Pull the wool over everyone's eyes including my own

I totally understand if you roll your eyes. God, church—you are probably thinking what does any of that have to do with hitting rock bottom? Well a lot actually. You see, I've always believed in God (even when I was running from Him). The reality is that God has done a lot more believing in me than I have in Him at times. But the people of this church—they get it!

You need to understand that I have a great depth of faith in God and a much shallower belief in religion. For me, life is about loving God and loving people. God loves us for who we are and wants to help us have better, more peaceful, productive, less dramatic, and devastating lives. It's so important to have a good support system, and the people of my church have been so amazing in their acceptance of me and their loving ability to be able to see people through God's eyes.

When I reconnected with the church, I was certain it wasn't supposed to happen like this. It was right after this time when I said that I would never attend church regularly again—let alone be a member of one—but I got involved in the ministry and found myself making friends and actually confiding in a few new people.

I learned from those who had dealt with some of the same issues I had—including the fact that if I wanted my life to be better, more stable, and more consistent I need to start working on it again. So I asked the pastor of this church if we could meet together, and we did. I had already told him pieces of my story. He and his wife helped me through pretty tough relationship issues in my life before this visit to his office.

In this meeting, I sat down with Pastor and told him that I had come as far as I knew how to come on my own, that I didn't know where to go from here in getting my mental and emotional health back on track. I thought it was time for me to call in the cavalry (couldn't bring myself to say the words therapist or counselor that day).

I knew it wouldn't be easy. I wasn't as far away from that slippery, manipulative person that I used to be as I am now. Truth be told, I was jaded and scared and so afraid that no matter who I saw, the very first answer was going to be you need to be medicated. I was as untrusting of the psychological therapeutic process as anyone could be. Yet I knew that I didn't want to stay stuck where I was mentally and emotionally for the rest of my life.

I had a few basic requirements. It needed to be a Christian counselor. I needed the pastor to understand if I felt like I needed to bail, it didn't mean that I didn't want to do this. Most of all, I needed to know that he wouldn't be offended because I knew if it didn't feel right, I was going to get out of Dodge and fast!

So the pastor said he knew of this therapist that I should try. Local, straight shooting—the actual sentence he said was this: "Aim, I really believe this guy is the real deal." Then he added a disclaimer: "If it doesn't work out, we'll keep working together until we find the right fit." Pastor was pretty confident that I should set up an appointment.

I did. I went through all the normal stuff—scheduling the appointment, telling Pastor I scheduled the appointment (it's important that you have people in your life who know your treatment plan and will check on you to keep you accountable), waiting for the appointment. Then before I knew it, it was the night before the session.

I didn't sleep at all that night, didn't tell my family I was going. I did mention it to my best friend. My appointment was first thing in the morning before work. I got out of bed that morning in tears. I couldn't do it. I've been out of therapy for so long, and I haven't had to go back to therapy. So why start now?

Here's the thing. People refer to rock bottom like it's a one place, and when you hit it, you are automatically ready to start the hard work. It's not like that at all.

When you are sure you are ready to make the change, there are several levels to it. Keep in mind I'm not a therapist or anything, but here's how it went for me:

1. I knew something needed to change.
2. I wanted my life to be better.
3. I started making changes that were uncomfortable.
4. I'd back off and look around and try to figure out why it wasn't working.
5. I still wanted my life to be better.
6. I was afraid to move forward and fail again.

It would go in cycles like that for years. But this time was different.

I've already told you that it was a rough morning that morning I started therapy, that I had to call my pastor's wife just to be able to make it through the door. What I can't tell you often enough is that the help helps, that I am working to make life better on every level possible. I take the meds, I show up for the talk therapy, and I journal on my own. That doesn't count the music and the coloring and the just being honest at every opportunity.

3

Walking through the Therapist Door Again Years Later

So I was sitting outside the office. I had my pad folio with all the forms I'd printed from the website. I had the tears tucked away for the moment and was literally shaking. Prior to walking into this office (almost a decade ago), I had worked with four therapists (at different times in life) on a regular basis and several more therapists and counselors through inpatient, group, and intensive outpatient program settings. It's been years, but it's always the same thing.

In the past, I've worked with these professionals, knowing that therapy wouldn't do anything, and even then I was convinced this wasn't going to work—even as I was sitting here. Regardless I had been going over things in my head, trying to diffuse the landmines that would come up in this first session before I'd even met the man. I was sitting there, rehearsing the detailed patient history I was going to give and was trying to be ready for everything that could happen.

I kept repeating "She said I can do this!" in my head over and over as I took a seat in this quiet downstairs waiting area—the radio playing soft, nondescript music—when the therapist walked in and introduced himself.

I should probably point out here that I almost didn't make it through the door. I was on my way and was having a panic attack and had to pull over in the parking lot of a gas station and call my pastor's wife to get enough strength to move forward. There were parts of that conversation when I was literally crying so hard that she couldn't hear me. You see, my pastor recommended this guy, claimed that he was "the real deal" and that he's a counselor that "gets it."

I have to admit that because I was referred to him by my pastor, I didn't do any research at all on him. I made a point of *not* reading his profile on the group website. I had decided that I was just going to put on my big-girl boots and trust the referral I had received and go from there. I was not sure what I expected, but it wasn't what was in front of me. And I really didn't think it would take years to get to the place where I was ready to face life on my own.

We walked upstairs through this other waiting room; this one had a water cooler and some books and a table for kids to play and a few doors, one of which went into his office.

A desk, desk chair, and two couches (I had this whole snarky "shrink's couch" conversation going on in my head that I kept to myself and made me laugh on the inside a bit, but I think that was my own way of breaking the stress) were in this room that I was thankful wasn't brightly lit because I was already feeling like I looked like a train wreck as I walked through the door.

I would love to sit here and give you a play by play of that first session, but to be candid, it wasn't what I expected at all. It was really a blur. Here's what I know:

I sat down and forgot every single thing that I had been rehearsing for weeks and didn't know what to say. I do know I had told him that once upon a time, I was misdiagnosed years ago with bipolar and correctly diagnosed with borderline personality disorder. I know I was shocked when he didn't flinch or break eye contact or lose his professionalism for a moment and, in a very noncondescending way, empathized with what I had been through. Not only was I not expecting that, but I literally wasn't ready for it.

See, what I knew as I was starting this last round of talk therapy was that BPD is looked down on widely throughout the psychotherapeutic community. So what happened next sent me reeling.

The therapist then told me that he had done a great deal of work in everything I just told him about. He has actually lead groups of those who had been misdiagnosed as bipolar and done a lot of work with BPD. *Wait! What? Really?*

Even now, I remember looking at him and asking him to say that again. My new therapist saw the look on my face and informed me that my pastor (the one who referred me) didn't know any of this at the time that he referred me.

So yes! For those of you who question why I believe in God, it's because of things just like this.

You don't find out until you have been diagnosed and start to research borderline personality disorder how even the professionals who are supposed to support and treat and help you will look down on you once you have been diagnosed with BPD.

I realize that it may seem like a harsh and generalized statement. On several levels, it is, and I totally admit that. But I also admit, on a personal level, that part of the reason that statement is true—or at least was true on my account—is because I was shifty by nature. I hid things and was notorious for bolting when things get tough. I also knew how to work a person or a room to get the desired response, good or bad.

At this point, my head was reeling. I was trying to stay in the moment, which was really hard because all I wanted to do was head out the door. Then the therapist laid this on me: "It's up to you if you want to do this or not. I can tell you what will probably happen if you schedule another appointment. You'll probably keep it and perhaps a few more after that. Then things will get more difficult. You will most likely hide stuff. You may start to be late and then skip an appointment or two and then decide you want to just give up on the process altogether." He actually said to me, "No one can make you do this."

We scheduled another session and then I walked out that door and down the steps and out the other door and sat down in my car and called my pastor's wife. And I told her that I did it. I went through with it. Then I started to try to process everything. I had thirty-five minutes to get to work which was about a ten-minute drive. That gave me twenty minutes to think and five minutes to pull myself back together. And then it hit me. *Hold on.* Did he just tell me that I'm going to bail?

But Pastor said this therapist was "the real deal." Those words echoed in my head. Now I was just angry. How dare he? (Pause.) I did just tell him that I had bailed on therapists (more than one) and had a history of not being straight with anyone and that I didn't have any idea of how to have any functional relationship at all.

This is the reality of the borderline personality disorder patient. No matter how bad you want things to change and be able to hear things like "I did in that appointment that day and not want to head for the hills," there is a good chance you will struggle with it on and off for years to come—until you're ready to do this. And to paraphrase the therapist on that first appointment, no one can make you want to cross the borderline enough to make you do it. *You* have to do more than just show up for the process. You have to be willing to do the work on your own. The therapist will guide you, but he or she can't make you go where you aren't willing to.

4

Borderline Personality Disorder (BPD)

So I've gone back and forth on this chapter. Do I make it more or less clinical? The reality of this book is that it's for everyone, and I am not a mental or emotional health professional. So if you are looking for in-depth, good resources on borderline personality disorder (BPD), go to www.nimh.nih.gov (National Institute of Mental Health) and look it up.

What you are about to read is definitely not the medical professional's definition and is definitely skewed by my own mental filter.

When you take all the jargon out of it, this is what it boils down to (my words here).

It's considered a serious thing to deal with. If you have it, you are marked with unstable moods, relationships, and behavior. Even with that all being true, it turns out that there is a stigma associated with the diagnosis—even in the medical community—because for some time, it was kind of thought to be a catch all diagnosis.

Some people who have been diagnosed with BPD have psychotic events, but that is because of some other diagnosis or condition and not really reflective of the borderline personality disorder. It was purposefully given a vague name because it was kind of a catch-all diagnosis that may have initially not necessarily had a specific set of criteria which defined it. Clear as mud. Right?

Well the long story made short is that folks with BPD have to deal with not being able to (or at least feeling as if they cannot) regulate or control thoughts; emotions; reckless, impulsive, dangerous behavior; and relationships that are volatilely unstable—really unstable. I mean one minute it's "I love you and need you" and the next it's "you repulse me," then "I need you" again.

There are also a lot of other issues that can occur at the same time: depression; anxiety; addiction; self-esteem; even going the level of self-mutilation and suicidal thoughts, behaviors, and actually jumping off the planet.

There are nine signs and symptoms of BPD. In order to *carry* the diagnosis, you have to have at least five of them. Because of this fact; it's somewhat of a transient diagnosis—which is to say that literally one day you can have it and one day later not so much and a month later it's back again.

That's that part that makes it so overwhelming—because the whole mental and emotional health thing doesn't always come with a definition. It's not like cancer or a heart attack or a stroke. There isn't a test or a scan that will say definitively that this is what you have, so deal with it.

And even when you are certain that this is what you have, there's no standard treatment plan, which is to say that it varies due to how many (and which) symptoms you show. Because of that, every single case is so different that it's hard to even find text (as a lay person) that will really help me understand what I am going through.

At the time of my initial diagnosis (back when I was misdiagnosed as having bipolar disorder), I carried nine of nine symptoms, and I would for years to come.

I didn't know how to deal with it. I was embarrassed and felt like some kind of freak or monster, especially after I got out of the locked adult mental health unit. I could only speak for me, but it didn't magically become less embarrassing because I voluntarily admitted myself.

So here is the short list of the nine. It's the list I'm able to keep in my head which—as I'm writing this—helps me to make sure that I'm saying on the right path:

1. Extreme reactions to abandonment (weather actual or perceived)
2. Pattern of erratic and unstable relationships—with the same relationship going back and forth between love and worship to dislike and anger, then back to being close again
3. Distorted self-image (either overinflating or devaluing), which can result in sudden changes in mood, plans, and what you believe
4. Dangerous or impulsive behaviors (i.e. sex, spending, behaviors of addiction, etc.)
5. Suicidal threats, behaviors, and self-harming behaviors that occur again and again
6. Intensely fluctuating moods—each mood lasting anywhere from days to hours
7. Inappropriate and intense anger issues
8. Feeling alone and bored to a degree where it always feels this way; there is a desperation to this
9. Having stress-related paranoid thoughts or extreme feelings of isolation (i.e. feeling like you are seeing yourself from across the room) and aren't at one with yourself.

That's the list as I tend to recall it. There is a much more in depth and accurate list on the NIMH website, or you can talk to your doctor or a mental health professional. Believe it or not, it's really hard to sit here and tell the world that, at one time, I had all nine of those issues going for me at once. But it's true.

By the time I made it to the psychologist's office whom I've been seeing as I write the majority of this book, I was barely borderline, which goes back to the fact that you have to carry at least five of the nine symptoms to technically carry the disorder as a diagnosis.

I can tell you with 100-percent accuracy that when I was initially diagnosed (when I had all nine symptoms at once), I didn't see it as a disorder or an issue. When I was diagnosed as having borderline personality disorder, everything that was classified as a symptom I classified as normal, and it was for me.

I lived that way for a long time, and when I received the diagnosis, I wasn't ready to change any of it. Granted I was misdiagnosed with the bipolar disorder, but I was broken and didn't know where to start to try and fix things.

It's all very dark and cloak and dagger—the dark stigma that surrounds issues of mental and emotional health. When I started this last round of talk therapy, I was fortunate enough to most of the time carry less than the five symptoms that are required for the borderline diagnosis. It wasn't always that way, and to this day, there is still a stigma that surrounds the fact that I've been in a locked unit or on psych meds or suicidal in the past.

That's why I feel that it's so important to start to educate and discuss issues as they occur. If I had kept everything in the dark, I would never be ready to start a journey that would culminate with me crossing the borderline.

5

Bipolar

Before we start this chapter, there are some things you need to know.

1. There are people out there who really have this condition.
2. There are people out there who have lost the battle with this condition (I have friends who have died because of it).
3. If you need the meds, take the meds.
4. If you feel like you're okay and you're on the meds, stay on the meds; it probably means they are working.
5. If you get busted for going off your meds or find yourself struggling while on your meds, tell your doctor. (It really does help!)

With all that being said:
You never realize how much passion you really have or how many emotions you are holding onto about something until you sit down to write it out for the sole purpose of sharing it with the world.

This chapter—it scares me quite a bit. It comes with a lot of anger and even some guilt, which is kind of ironic considering the fact that hindsight is 20/20. And when I was in the middle of it, I was clueless to what was really going on.

The borderline had me, and without knowing it, I was embracing the symptoms of something I didn't even know that I had. As a result, I wasn't sleeping (more than one or two hours a night on average), was lying, self-medicating with alcohol (even after the DUI), and had some form of every other symptom on the list above and felt like it was normal behavior.

I was diagnosed with something called bipolar (aka manic-depressive illness). I'm not a mental health expert. Actually I probably know just a little more about it right now than what it would take to be dangerous. So before we head out of the gate, please allow me to direct anyone who wants real information on bipolar disorder to start where I now start all my research on mental health topics begins; The National Institute of Mental Health (http://www.nimh.nih.gov).

Look up bipolar, and you will find that this illness is caused by an imbalance of chemicals in the brain. That there are different types of bipolar disorder, and the differences in types are marked by numbers. That those who are affected by the disorder experience a rollercoasterlike series of highs and lows that can be both cyclical and or sporadic, depending on the type of bipolar disorder that they have.

This is another disorder that can be diagnosed in combination with other disorders or mental and emotional health conditions. I can tell you that I wasn't properly diagnosed. I can tell you that a great portion of the list of reasons that happened had to do with who I was at the time.

I can tell you that this is a real disorder and that the people who are affected with it spend their entire lives, trying to deal and cope and find ways to function. If you are looking for me to give you more information than that. You've come to the wrong person.

At the point in time when I was diagnosed, I hadn't learned to be my own advocate yet. So what happened was that someone told me that I had this bipolar disorder, which I had never heard of at the time. The very first thing I did was run out and buy a book on it, even before I started on the meds. It was one of those true story books about someone who not only had to deal with the illness but overcame it and began helping others. Then came the meds. It was over a series of years and always combinations—

never just a single tablet or capsule a day—but the combinations and side effects were crazy. Here's at least a partial list in no particular order:

- Serzone 150 mg, twice daily
- Xanax 0.25 mg, thrice daily as needed; changed to 0.5 mg, thrice daily as needed
- Serax 10 mg every 6 hours as needed
- Eskalith (lithium) 450 mg, twice daily
- Depakote 250 mg, thrice daily; changed to 500 mg in the morning, 250 mg as needed, and at bedtime
- Trazodone 100 mg, one-half at bedtime
- Ambien 10 mg at bedtime
- Lexapro 10 mg, each day
- Ativan 0.5 mg, thrice daily
- Klonopin 1 mg: one-fourth tab twice daily and one-half at bedtime
- Effexor 75 mg each morning
- Narvane 3 mg, thrice daily
- Lamictal 200 mg at bedtime
- Vistaril 25 mg at bedtime as needed
- Risperidone 2 mg, twice daily
- Wellbutrin 200 mg in the morning
- Zyprexa 20 mg at bedtime
- Geodon 60 mg, twice daily
- Abilify 15 mg at bedtime
- Seroquel: 100 mg at dinner, 3-100 mg pills at night, 25 mg (one to two) as needed for headaches
- Fluoxetine 20 mg at bedtime

This is the list that I could remember, and I got some help from my med doc's office. But I know there are a few that are missing. Here's how the meds went for me.

(I'm phobic of needles to a crazy degree, so it's important for me to let you know that as I'm writing this, I'm on an antidepressant and an anxiety med that don't require blood tests. If they did require blood tests, I would still take them because they really work for me. It would just be a harder and more involved process.)

The meds on that list are in no particular order and were taken in combinations that varied widely and wildly over a series of several years.

Initially (before I was diagnosed) I was prescribed an antidepressant by my family doc. I was in counseling and the depression was getting worse and not better. Things kept rolling downhill until I found myself with my first emergent admission in a local hospital's locked adult mental health unit.

This admission wasn't meant to do anything other than keep me from hurting myself and getting me back to being functional and safe enough to be let out with real people. It was here that I had my first baseline blood test, and they started with a series of medicines that required regular blood tests.

Before I got out of this facility, I had to have plans to meet with both a talk therapist and a psychiatrist (psych med doc). It didn't really matter if I was starting on meds or if I was changing meds; there would typically be one of three things that happened.

- I started taking the medication, and it started to work right away.
  - I knew they were working. They had to be working. He or she said this would work. I wasn't sleeping, but they were working, right?
- I started taking the meds, and nothing happened (in the first couple of days).
  - Frequently I was warned that this might happen—that it takes a few days, weeks, or in some cases, a couple of months for levels to build up in the bloodstream and the body to adjust.

- I would take the meds but wouldn't be totally compliant.
  - I would "try" to take the meds and maybe skip a dose here and there. The meds would make me feel different—funny and not in a good way. I would tell the docs and therapists that I was taking them.

(Here's a tip for you. Most of the time, even the bad therapists and docs—the ones who grab the script pad first for everything—can tell when you're not taking your meds. It really doesn't matter how good of an actor you are or what you do or say to try to convince them.)

And so it goes, then begins the cycle. The meds work for a few weeks then we tweak them and do more blood tests and then we change them all together.

The thing with the meds I was on is that they were the big guns. They don't carry side effects for everyone, but they did for me. (This is one of those parts of the book that's really hard to compare to).

The side effects are scarier when you are looking at the list I'm about to type than they actually were when I was on them. I could go down the entire list but I don't really want to, so I'll go with the one that affected me the most and the one that was most noticeable to anyone around me.

The one that was hardest for me to deal with was the fact that the combination of meds I was on slowed me down. The only way I know to describe it is that I was like living like through marshmallows, or maybe it was close to those scenes in television shows and movies that are in super slow motion. It might seem like that would make life easier, but actually it changed a lot of things for me. My attention span became shorter (not that it was ever super long). It caused issues for me at work, and when it came to my personal life, I couldn't keep up with the lies I told myself and others. It caused other issues. I was tired all the time and didn't feel up to doing the day-to-day things that keep the world moving. Two good examples would be oral and personal hygiene. Now those were two things that suffered greatly for quite some time.

The one that was hardest for those around me to watch was something that I called the jitters. My hands would constantly be shaky, and my legs would constantly bounce when I was sitting without my thinking about it. It would make people feel nervous. Although they wouldn't say anything (and it was rare for someone to bring it up), I would choose to believe that meant that their not noticing would mean they didn't know, or I would tell myself that some people have ticks. Even now when I'm on my meds (more frequently when I'm not), when I get super stressed, my left upper eyelid twitches. It has only happened twice since I started taking the Remeron. This wasn't that type of muscle movement.

This was every single time I sat down. I would slide my foot backward so that (if you took a yard stick and put it at the center of my knee joint on either side) the ball of my foot would be behind my knee (on the floor) and then my leg bounced while the ball of my foot remained on the floor. If you think of the game adults play sometimes with kids, where the child straddles the adult, and the adult holds the child and starts to bounce his leg. It's kind of like that only there's no real desire to bounce your leg at all.

At times, the hands would tremble so badly that it was hard to eat but because in that moment, as long as the med doc felt that the conditions the medication was designed to treat were more under control, the rest of it was just basically collateral damage and something I needed to learn to live with.

There really is a list, and the list is both deep and wide. And who knows? Maybe it will be for another book. The thing is the bipolar disorder was a misdiagnosis, and the correct diagnosis would have been low self-esteem and borderline personality disorder. The craziest part of all this was that I was misdiagnosed by professionals and correctly diagnosed by a man in his seventies who never heard of or really thought about any of this before he met me.

When you need the meds, you really need the meds (take it from me because I now know it's true). The bipolar thing—it's real. I have friends who deal with it. Some of them are very diligent and successful; some aren't. I've seen it destroy marriages, families, and even take lives.

You have to take things one step at a time and be honest with yourself and learn how to advocate for yourself, define yourself, and not let someone else tell you who you are. If you can find a way to even start doing that, you greatly increase your chances of crossing the borderline.

5.5

Bipolar—Here Is What I Should Have Written

Today in a conversation I had with my therapist, I was taken back to a time when I was very different. The chapter on bipolar was already written and was in first draft form, but there are a few things I should totally confess.

1. My brain is wired differently (when I'm not on any medication; this is how God made me, and it's not a bad thing)—not just a little differently but a lot differently. Without the Remeron, I can hold six conversations in my mind at once, go on little to no sleep for days at a time, and have more energy than I would have if I were riding a roller coaster while doing it. This is just part of who I am.
2. When I was diagnosed as bipolar, I presented as a textbook case. Literally I could have been the dictionary definition, even to the point of having extra perception in some areas. I remember being able to walk into a room or down the street and hear every single noise, every single conversation, and keep track of them all—feeling like they were each coming in on their own channel of my brain as if my brain was a was a soundboard.
3. When I was misdiagnosed, I ran out and grabbed the first book I could find by an author who not only had the diag-

nosis, but beat it. And from that book, I learned how to embrace the diagnosis and the symptoms that caused me to present as the poster gal for bipolar.

Today in therapy, I so wanted to be angry with those who diagnosed me, treated me, and medicated me, but it turns out this is one of those areas where I have to take my own level of responsibility for.

You know by now that I have had admissions—more than one—to adult, locked psych units. What I'm not sure I've conveyed clearly is that bipolar (much like borderline personality disorder) is a hard diagnosis to hear, harder to accept, and even harder to do the work on treating it.

It's an actual diagnosis. I know people who carry the diagnosis, and I can tell you that meds (when properly prescribed) and talk therapy and behavior modification can make a world of difference. If you have the condition, meds are definitely a part of a process that can change things for you.

My issue was that I didn't have the condition, so I literally spent years trying to fix something that didn't exist. I didn't know how to be honest about what I was going through or even understand what it was, so I didn't know how to be my own advocate.

The doc said, "Based on your symptoms, this is what you have/who you are." And I ran with it. Years were spent going on and off medications never less than three at a time. I was always being told by my psychiatrist, "We'll get it right" and "It's just a varying version of bipolar." I know in all the years I was medicated, there was never a solid four months where I was on the same meds at the same doses and administration times.

Yet I know people who have this disorder. *I know the right meds do help when you stay compliant!* I also know meds are just part of the treatment for this disorder that can cost people their lives.

I know that there is shame that is associated with taking psych meds and having to go to therapy or to a doctor, let alone a locked unit to get your meds adjusted because you don't feel safe. I've seen the high energy and confidence and feeling of connection lead to feeling depressed and alone and suicidal even when someone is in a room surrounded by people who truly love and care about him or her.

I've seen the dysfunctional become functional, and I've also witnessed the functional become dysfunctional because the medication is working so well they feel they don't need it any more. I've attended funerals of those who couldn't wrap their mind around the fact that the meds help and the therapy helps and that you can't give up on getting better just because it feels like you already are.

Bipolar—manic depression is just what it sounds like. Deep dark sadness for every reason or no reason, then all of a sudden, energy and euphoria and all the craziness that comes with it.

What I should have written in that last chapter was that just because I don't have it doesn't mean that it doesn't exist. It does and it hurts and it destroys relationships and lives and there is a stigma attached to it, but if you are dedicated to figuring out what's going on and determined to make life better with medication and therapy, you can do just that! It can be done, and it's not something that anyone should have to do alone.

So my hope is that these two chapters let us start the discussion of how to change lives by learning and listening and educating and not just hiding and giving up. It's time to end the stigma surrounding mental and emotional Ill-being and start living life. To do that, you have to talk about the stuff like bipolar and borderline personality disorder and schizophrenia and all the other things that are so "uncommonly" normal.

Mental illness and emotional Ill-being affects many more people than you think. So don't hide it because unless you shine a light on something and examine it, you never will know what it is or how to deal with it.

6

What's in Your Backpack?

You will see me referring to this chapter several times as you make your way through this book. The reason for that is probably because it is one of the easiest lessons to learn but one of the hardest to accept.

It directly relates to me walking into a therapist's office knowing that I have gone as far as I can on my own. I wouldn't admit it out loud but I knew that I'm kind of intelligent (or at least that's what others think of me), but I also knew that the stuff I knew would not let me become the person I was meant to be.

So one session, the backpack theory was explained to me.

It's as if when we are born, we are given this theoretical backpack that we will carry with us for our entire life. At first, I have to admit it sounded pretty cool because I didn't learn how to be a good student, but I rocked out the "select a new backpack at the beginning of every year" thing.

Then comes the significance of this particular backpack, and things start to fall apart because it turns out I have carried this backpack with me through life, filling it with lessons and homework and emotional responses. Things like the following:

- Self-esteem
- Manners
- Body image
- What you allow yourself to feel

- How you process information
- How you express feelings and emotions
- What you can and cannot do
- Who you can and cannot trust

The list goes on from there. Here's the thing about the backpack. Unlike the ones you have picked out for school or your favorite handbag or briefcase, the one we are issued at birth kind of is the same for everyone. When you are born and you are placed into the arms of your first care giver, that is the moment that things start to change and we all begin to learn who we are.

You see, the stuff that gets put into the backpack is based on the people you trust to teach you and help you. The folks that we are taught as children to believe were the white hats (i.e. parents, teachers, presidents, fireman, soldiers, pastors, medical professionals); they all have backpacks too that are filled with the lessons they've learned. The lessons they have learned all start out with filters that are developed from the people from which they have learned their lessons. Those lessons fill the backpacks of the people who have taught us.

So if they have had bad teachers, they are likely giving out bad lessons and homework. Basically in its own way, it's the "history repeats itself" thing.

If someone grows up in an environment where his or her authority figure demeans others when he or she is feeling bad about his or herself, there is a good chance that the person growing up may develop the same characteristic. They may not realize they have that trait, and more important (to the life they lead and how they treat others), they may not see anything wrong with the cycle.

So you learn how to deal with life based on what you've been taught. When I started this last round of talk therapy, my backpack was filled with bad stuff. The reason I couldn't finish crossing the borderline on my own is because I never realized the lessons that were in this backpack were in direct opposition to healthy relationships, positive self-esteem, and respect for others.

So that day, when I walked into my pastor's office and said that I had come as far as I could on my own, it turns out that I had come a little farther than I thought I did. I didn't know about the backpack theory yet, but I had figured out that all people are God's creation and deserve respect and love. That's something I relearned on my own; that lesson wasn't handed to me to complete.

It turns out that examining these lessons and the contents of this backpack isn't something that is going to end when I'm through with the therapy sessions. Actually it is something that I'll have to keep an eye on every day for the rest of my life, even after the borderline is far behind me.

7

Why Bother? And How It All Starts

I sort of addressed this in the preface of this book, but after a few conversations I've had in the past few days, I think that it bears a deeper look. Why would anyone ever write a book that talks about what it's really like to go through the process of talk therapy, medication, and trying to rebuild a broken life? What is it that takes someone from the place of being broken to being healed enough to be willing to put his or herself out there? I could take the high road and come up with some flowery and eloquent answer, but here's the truth.

The place I came from was broken. Don't misunderstand that to mean that I grew up in what's known as a broken home. My parents are still married as both sets of my grandparents were for their entire lives. I went to church and was what I now believe was a relatively good kid growing up. I didn't do drugs or drink.

But by the time I hit thirty, here is what was in the wake of my lifeboat:

- An arrest for driving under the influence that was fast tracked and would later be expunged, came after a lot of self-medicating of emotional pain with alcohol
- A failed marriage
- A resume that was impressive in skills but not in length of stay at a job
- Unstable relationships with everyone I knew

- I walked away from God by walking away from church
- Multiple scars on my body from cutting
- Being more mentally and verbally cruel to myself
- Agreeing to a misdiagnosis and being on the wrong medications for almost a decade
- Lying
- Manipulating
- That doesn't even include the physical and sexual abuse

It's a very valid question. When you finally have things on track and you don't have to deal with these kinds of issues anymore and you know it's time to move forward, why would you ever write a book like this one?

The answer is simple for me. I didn't get the answers to how to deal with everything on my own. I didn't know where or why or how to look for real help. I met a friend who agreed to only be my friend if the lying stopped, and I started being honest about who I was. Years later, I had a direct supervisor who called me out on not addressing things right away and not addressing them to the person with whom I had the issue. The person interviewing me for this position told me that if I was going to be her employee, it had to stop immediately. God put a lot of people in my path who would help me learn how to be a better me. I can't sit here and not pay it forward. I know how much it hurts to be lost and alone and unstable. I know how much I hated myself when I felt like a monster, I knew how much of a freak I felt like, and I could never really tell you why.

I know it's not in everyone to do this, and I know I'm not even in the end zone of the things that God has in store for me yet. On the bad days, I know that if I can make it through the next five minutes, there will be five after that and then another and another, and eventually the first five minutes that seemed so horrible will just be a memory.

I know that my friends and family haven't always known or understood what has gone on with me. How could they? The reason I ask is because I didn't understand me.

So that's the answer. I want people who are going through what I went through and what I continue to go through now as my own friends and my own advocates and as people who are standing up as advocates so that those who are in need of better mental and emotional health can have someone they can relate to.

Believe it or not, that was the easy question and answer. Here comes the hard part.

So my guess is the next question is how do you do it? How do you get started? How do you go from being a lying and manipulative person to someone who is dependable, known for truth, and facing things head on? You just start doing it.

For me, even now years later, it frequently means picking your battles. It means not opening your mouth for the expressed purpose of hurting someone back because they have just chosen to hurt you. It means choosing to not push someone away because they are trying to help.

I was in a situation last night where I went to the hospital to visit a friend who was fighting a tough battle of infection. After that, I had a viewing to attend. I just finished visiting a friend, walked down the long hospital corridor, found a seat, and just took a minute. There were these huge windows that looked down over the city that the hospital was in. I just sat down to take a minute and breathe, and all of a sudden, my eyes started leaking. Not full-out crying—but I was tearing up and trying so hard to stay strong, hoping no one would see my weakness.

This couple I knew from church walked up while I was in tears. They didn't say anything. She just laid a hand on my shoulder. All I could say in that moment, without exploding into tears, was, "I just needed a minute." I promise you even as I write this, I know that I did the best I could to keep it together for those few minutes yesterday. I was fighting it hard, and those tears were the seams coming unglued.

It didn't last long, and it wasn't even five minutes until it was over. But when she laid her hand on my shoulder, she and her husband prayed for me. Now if you're not a Christ follower, that may not mean much to you, but let me tell you something. To have someone agree with you and tell you that you can make it without trying to fix what you're going through—that's more than most people ever get! To have someone tell you that you can make it and that God is fighting with you and not against you—it's hard for me to wrap my head around anyone refusing that. So yeah, I could have said that I was fine and that it was okay and I was just resting. And at best, that may have been partially true. Instead I just said, "I just needed a minute before I moved on." And that was enough.

It doesn't always work that way. There are going to be several times—as you find your own answers—when facing things head on does nothing more than get you ensnared in a bear trap. I could recount dozens of times that it did for me, and I can only tell you to not stop facing things. It gets easier to own both the bad and the good. It worked for me. Now I'm more afraid of not facing things head on and getting caught in a lie and ruining the reputation that I've started to build. Not to mention that it's nice to not have an agenda or an attack plan.

For me, the bad stuff was the easiest to own. The good stuff was harder because I didn't see myself as a good person. God made me. God's Word says that He not only knows who I am, but He also loves me. So yeah, I do my best to keep facing the truth. It turns out the truth is good and by far better than the alternative!

8

You've Got a Decision to Make

Even now—before you start the next chapter in the book you have a decision to make—by now, you may have decided that this isn't really for you, you're totally enthralled, or you feel rather indifferent to the content. As a result, you can either move forward in reading this book or put it down and walk away.

Choosing to be an advocate for you own mental health (or mental health of a loved one) can be a lot like that. You have a choice to make, and unlike the reading of this book, it's not a once-and-done kind of thing. It's a decision that has to be made every single minute of every day.

The thing is, unlike the reading of a book which can be done in secret, mental and emotional healing issues are something that you live out loud every day even if you don't tell anyone you are doing them. There is a lot of safety in the familiar, and if you're anything like me, you feel like you have let yourself and others down. So it can be hard, stressful, and cause anxiety to even try to imagine a world where you are successful, happy, and loved.

It's not familiar. Since I've started to bring this process out into the light instead of hiding it in the shadows, I've been asked several questions. Probably the one that I get the most is this: "I don't understand why they (my loved one) just won't change?"

It's not as easy as it looks on the TV shows or in the movies. I wish I had one answer that would cover everything, but I don't. I can tell you that I have had friends who have been abandoned for the choices they have made (good, bad, right, wrong) and have been judged harshly.

Everything from lifestyle decisions, deciding to take meds, or go for talk therapy, etc.—it's not an easy thing; this working on getting all healed and becoming a complete person again. There's a lot more to it than anyone who hasn't been through it knows. I've seen more people lose the battle and their life because it couldn't be done than I care to admit.

So there are all kinds of decisions to be made. Do I go for help? Do I not go for help? Do I start meds (start meds again), or why even bother? Do I support my friend who has decided to go to therapy and take meds?

I heard questions raised about the fact that therapy isn't of God and neither is medication. I totally disagree with that. It's all a matter of who you know. I have been both wrongly and properly medicated and am honest enough to say that I played a big part in both of those things. God gives us doctors and therapists who know their stuff, but there are also a lot of medical professionals out there who aren't as good as they need to be.

This friend of mine frequently quotes to me a verse from the Bible that says, "My people perish for lack of knowledge." God wants us to advocate for ourselves. That means that God wants us to make decisions. He's a really good Father and wants us to love ourselves.

So it's really up to you. Do you want to pick up this book again and learn more about what it's like to go through the process of gaining self-esteem and good mental and emotional health, or do you want to put the book down and just ignore it and risk losing a battle you didn't even know you needed to fight? For me, the decision has become a simple, every day one. I don't know about you, but I have chosen to go ahead and cross the borderline!

9

Shifting the Perception of Normal

Normal ... The irony of that which is "normal" is that it is rarely defined for everyday people by anything other than everyone's own personal standard. I am not some movie star or politician or athlete or minister. I wake up in the morning and try to start my day just like everyone else. It's an any-day thing that turned into an everyday thing rather quickly as I started to restructure my life. The thing is that I never even realized that I defined normal until the moment that I had to tell a therapist what my definition of normal was.

My definition of normal starts with a big if:

If I sleep at night, when I open my eyes in the morning and think about what I have to do—let's say go to work—I think, "Well I need the paycheck." And I think about what obtaining that requires. Then the usual—chat it out with God; bathe; brush my teeth; do my hair, clothes, and maybe makeup. A few days ago I started to examine the conversation that takes place every day, and listened to myself as I planned out my day in my own mind.

It starts with me taking a segment of my drive time and lining up tasks that need to be done, and in the same thought train, I am thinking of how I have let everyone down by not having things already completed and how I have to do better to be liked or accepted. I have been told by those who know me best that I have the thought processes and sensitivity of an artist and a free thinker. However, there is also something in me that just really takes comfort in having rituals and routines—even the ones that are filled with self-condemnation.

Now here is normal as it's defined by professionals and generally by the rest of the world:

The dictionary defines normal as the following. I was blown away by the fact that the B definition is actually a psychological definition.

- A. Approximately average in any psychological trait as intelligence, personality, or emotional adjustment
- B. Free from any mental disorder; sane

At this point in my life, I have done a bit of studying on the subject not only as it relates to me, but also as it relates to people that I know. With all the research I've done and with the folks I've talked with about these things, I've come to one conclusion. The textbook definition or at least the dictionary definition of normal really isn't so normal. Actually it's rather extraordinary!

I would challenge you to find a person who has never been depressed or in denial, someone who hasn't suffered abuse or abandonment. Go ahead and try to find someone who has never been introverted or tried too hard to be liked by everyone, or just try to find someone who hasn't acted like everything was just fine when it wasn't or someone who hasn't hidden from the world because it's a dark and scary place.

I submit to you that being normal isn't normal. Yet there is such an affection and respect for normal things that it has caused a huge stigma that is associated with things that are not "normal." So we don't talk about things like the following:

- ❏ Abuse
- ❏ Mental illness
- ❏ Going to therapy or going on/taking psych meds
- ❏ Suicidal thoughts

The list goes on from there. If normal isn't normal, then maybe it's time to redefine it or to take being abnormal out of the shadows and into the light because it's a lot more normal than you think. And seeing it and talking about it are the only ways you can cross the borderline.

10

Medication Stigmata

This is a chapter I wish someone would have given me eighteen years ago. It would have saved me so much time and hassle and heartache and could have even saved me from having a criminal record (driving under the influence) as well.

There is this stigma associated with taking psych meds. All types of medications are so accessible here, and it's easy to take meds for granted. At the exact same time and for the same condition, you may hear someone say, "Well I'm only on this medication" or "I have to take nine pills a day."

Personally, I found myself this winter trying to stay off antibiotics because I don't want to become resistant, and I've been on several courses in the past few years due to respiratory issues. But there is a stigma that's much worse when you talk about psych meds.

The thing is, no one tells you the pitfalls or that there's this cycle to it. You go into therapy for whatever reason—usually pushed into it by someone or some event. You may not think you have a problem, or you may wind up in a locked unit on a voluntary commit or committed by a doc, therapist, or peace officer. How you get to the medicine isn't so important. The med doc, therapist, etc., listen to you tell your story once or twice, and it can be all truth or all lies—or a mix. Soon thereafter, you have some kind of diagnosis, but before they hand you a prescription for medication, they should tell you a lot of things, starting with some possibilities for the cycle. You'll be medicated or not. You'll tell them what they want to hear like, "I've taken all my meds and haven't missed a single dose." The medication may work for a while, then it won't or it will. And you will feel good, so you will think you don't need it anymore. Either way, you may decide to go off your meds and then it will all start over again.

When you get out of the mental healthcare facility or program you are in, your friends and your family will think that since you got out of the unit (frequently by playing the game and telling everyone in there what they wanted to hear), you're all fixed, but that is rarely the case.

It's a self-perpetuating cycle that is caused by all the stigma associated with mental and emotional ill-being. You see, ignorance and hate are as much of a disease as any medical diagnosis. I have seen both hate and ignorance lead to death. After I figured out that the bipolar disorder was wrong, I learned to be my own advocate. Years after that, I was so blessed to be referred into the treatment of a psychologist who knows his stuff.

After about two years of sessions with this therapist, I was at a point of crisis. All I knew was I couldn't sleep (for days in a row), and I couldn't get my brain to slow down. This was years after my initial misdiagnosis and being correctly diagnosed with BPD. I couldn't get it to stop. I didn't know what to do and knew I was really on the verge of not being safe enough to be able to say I was safe. Other than Ativan or Xanax for anxiety, I had not been on a psych med in years—more than seven. I had occasionally been given some stuff to try to help me sleep, but even those things were either an off label usage or a homeopathic item like melatonin or valerian.

Sleeping wasn't the only issue on this day in particular. It's the having six thoughts at once and not being able to finish any of them because they keep running into each other and knocking you off course.

My therapist knew the emotional *ledge* I was on and started to talk me off it by telling me that I needed to go on medication.

Immediately I started to wig out. *There was absolutely no way I was going to go back on psych meds after what happened when I was misdiagnosed.one anxiety med was okay* (and I was already on that). *It just wasn't going to happen. He could forget that.*

This happened during the time frame in which I was writing this book and, just to be clear (my friends, pastor, and others who know me will verify), at this point in my life when there is a problem I try face it head on. So I really wasn't mincing a lot of words (and frankly at this point even choosing them very carefully)—even more so after he even suggested meds.

So Doc needed to talk me off of that *ledge* I was on, and frankly the way he did it was rather remarkable.

He gave me two amazing scenarios that really took the sting out of having to be back on psych meds.

The first scenario involved beta blockers. Beta blockers are a cardiac (heart) medication. That is their primary purpose, but they also have this off-label usage where they are used to help people who have anxiety when speaking in public. The folks who are taking beta blockers for the public speaking thing—they aren't considered cardiac patients.

I heard him give the explanation. I was in tears and really didn't feel "crazy," but I was panicked because I remembered—remembered isn't the right word here—I knew what it was like when you were on the wrong medication, to feel trapped and not like yourself or even human. I just didn't feel like I was crazy, but I knew I couldn't get the thoughts to stop.

Then he told me that there are patients who have seizures who have to receive electric shock (cardioversion) to get their brain out of seizure mode.

Taking a medication to stop the thoughts from coming quite so fast and help me with sleep was kind of like that. He didn't think I was crazy or needed to carry some big psych diagnosis.

For me, it really softened the blow of it all. I went on this antidepressant called Remeron, which I am still on to this day, and if I'm blessed to have it slow down my brain like it has been, I will be blessed if I'm able to stay on it for the rest of my life.

So since Doc was able to tell me what I needed to know that day, I thought that I would let all of you know what I wish I would have been told eighteen years ago.

Are you ready? All buckled in? Here we go!

- This sucks.

Nothing anyone can say or do will change where are you at this moment. You have to find a way to move forward or at least fall back, so you can start again.

- You're not crazy, and this doesn't mean you are a freak or a monster.

Just because it feels that way right now doesn't mean it's true. We aren't always the best judge of our own effectiveness or even of the impact we have on those around us (which actually can be more of a good thing than bad).

- Find a way to tell the truth.

(This can be the hardest part if you are like I was and not used to being honest.)

Psychology isn't an exact science and is almost always made harder because you and I (the patient) are hiding all the stuff that will help us get a correct diagnosis and medication if needed. Telling partial truth or hiding who you are because you are embarrassed or ashamed really only prolongs the process by making it more difficult for everyone.

- Medication may not work the first time it's tried; it takes adjustments (sometimes several) and will make you feel off your game every time your body has to adjust to a new dosage.

There may or may not be blood tests (hundreds of them over time). The medication you're on may take a couple of months to become fully effective, so it may not seem like it's working. Or it may seem like it's working, then stop when you have full levels in your blood. It may make you feel sluggish or really clear headed.

- When it's working, you may feel lonely or angry or hurt, but that's because you have things to work on that don't have anything to do with the medication itself.

This is the hard part because feeling nothing or hiding behind what you want people to think you're feeling may feel better than this.

- When your medication is working well, you will feel like you don't need it.

You will want to not take it, toy with not taking it, and possibly even *(please learn from my mistakes, and don't do this)* stop taking it. It can be less effective when you get put back on it. You may need to start working with other meds if this happens because a lot of psych medications lose effectiveness when stopping and restarting occurs. You can build up a tolerance.

- When you stop taking the meds, the loneliness goes away, and you will be labeled by friends and family as noncompliant.

You'll hear things like "she must be off her meds" and be convinced every whisper in every room is about you. Ironically if you're on your meds and people know you are on meds, you will hear things like "she must not have taken her pill today" when you have normal responses to bad events.

- Taking medication doesn't make you a monster or a freak or a burden.

You should be proud of yourself for taking this step even if it feels like you shouldn't. It can take quite a while to figure everything out. Getting this straightened out to the place where you feel complete will always take more than just the medicine. There is a lot of learning and a lot of releasing that needs to be done. God made you, and you are some of His best work. And He loves you even when you don't love yourself.

- You're taking this med for a reason.

I'll be the first one to tell you that there are bad doctors and therapists out there who grab the prescription pad first thing or make snap diagnoses. In my opinion, these are the folks who should have their credentials revoked. You will, however (even when properly medicated), have a contingency of friends who are likely to tell you.

"You're such a nice person."
"You don't need that medication."
"Look at how well you are doing."
"You're going to be okay. You will be fine if you go off it."

It's important to remember that these people don't see all the stuff you are hiding, and they don't live with you 24/7. And even if they did, they still wouldn't see your thoughts.

- If you're off your meds, say you're off your meds. Doctors and therapists almost always know even if you don't tell them.

Not to mention there is a blood test or event coming up that will undoubtedly confirm it anyway. We get that you don't want to take meds (check out the title to the chapter). Not many people want to take meds, but trying to hide that you're not taking meds doesn't help anyone.

The biggest thing I wish I would have known early on about the process (and this sounds very elementary, but had I learned it early on it would have saved me a lot of lost years) It's not you against your psychology team. We all need to work together to get things working the way they should.

There is a good chance that the people around, the ones you've known for years, won't know what to do when things change for you, even if they change for the better. There are a series of actions and reactions that are, at this point in your life, programmed responses. Chances are you are manipulative. That sounds horrible, but I had to realize that everything we do is done for a reason, and more often than not, it is done to make life better for us in some (at time just perceived) way.

You'll make someone mad, so they leave you alone. You'll try to get close to someone you've just pushed away because you don't want to feel so lonely. You'll isolate because you don't want to infect the happy people.

It is okay not to be okay. You don't have to be okay all the time, and it is okay to ask for the help you need.

So I went on the psych med in my time of crisis. As I write this, the results are still in the short-term stage, but it's good. Really good! My thinking is clear; my sleep is better. There is a great deal of work that I still have to do—*Oh!*

Let's add two final things to the list of things you should be told before you start the medication.

- This isn't necessarily a life sentence.

Just because the medication that I'm on is really working for me and giving me clearer thinking than I had even as a small child and it is something that I'm not seeing myself wanting to give up as long as it works doesn't mean that what you're on, you'll have to be on forever. I believe that the fixing of mental and emotional issues happens on three different platforms:

1. Talk therapy
2. Spiritual
3. Medication

- The meds don't fix everything.

I still have work to do on behaviors, thought processes, and responses, but you know what? God loves me for who I am, and He put the therapist in my path who would give me guidance in how to talk to my medical doctor when I needed to go on medication. I take the pill every night at bedtime, and it's working well.

Now you should know that there are some people reading this book who will put it down thinking, "I'm a psych patient" or "I don't really need the medication." The thing is. I'm not psychotic or a psych patient or a freak or monster or any of the other things I've called myself over the years. The people around me—for the most part—like me, and you know what? I do need the medication. It helps. I have a lot of work to do, but I would rather take the meds than not deal with the reality of who I am. That alone, for me, is enough to make it worth taking the pill every night.

My suggestion to you is get the help. If you need the meds, take the meds. Find out who you really are and let yourself off the hook. You can't cross the borderline until you can at least see it for what it is.

11

It's Not Really about My Story

If you go back and reread the preface to this book, you will find that this book turned out to be a very different thing than I thought it would be. When I first sat down to write this, I thought it would be this tell-all of my past. It would define every single bad decision I made, show every mistake and wrongdoing, and be a calling out by name of the people who did me wrong.

It wasn't that I was vindictive or even proud of everything that had gone wrong in my life. To be transparent, more of the opposite was true. I had become this huge advocate for talking about things when it comes to mental health and was prepared to call myself out on the carpet for my defeats as well as take credit for my victories. Instead, this book had turned into more of a magnifying glass of the process. There was a possibility for success hiding in every failure, and every time I felt like I couldn't trust anyone because of who I am (or more correctly who I thought I was), God said, "I'm right here," even when I wasn't listening.

So today was Sunday. For me, this meant church, and even I had to admit that I was really feeling it today more than most days. Do you know what I mean?

Today was a good day. I didn't feel like a train wreck waiting to happen or like I was caught in the aftermath of some crazy life event. So I went and did my thing. We had a short review of music with the praise team (I play flute). Basically the band ran through the songs before service. Then I had a bit of down time before service began. Sunday morning church service began when we (as a church) sang and worshipped God, then announcements and Pastor got up to give the message.

Well today during worship it became increasingly evident that God is bigger—not just bigger than I am, but bigger than my mind could begin to comprehend or imagine. Normally that could be a bit distracting and, at times, even intimidating, but today it was just this thought in my head.

Pastor's message was about community and making all the pieces connect. He referenced 1 Peter chapter 2 from the Bible. If you've grown up in church it's probably a very familiar passage about being a chosen people. But today something that Pastor said made me stop right there in my seat. I started thinking of how God chose me. Actually the words in my head were a lot closer to "He picked me. He—God—the Creator of this whole entire universe … *He picked me!*"

You would think that would be the big shiny lesson or the icing on the spiritual cake, but it turned out that there was more in store for me this morning. I just kept thinking. At first, I start to think of the mistakes and the failures of life, of my story, of my misdiagnosis and the correct diagnosis and all the good stuff that's happened, but Pastor—he wasn't talking about my story.

The pastor was talking about community and connections. And still I kept thinking, *God picked me.* Then I remembered being that kid (which it turns out most of us at least feel like we were) standing in that line in gym class or on the playground with two children standing there facing me as I waited to be picked for a team and hoped against all hope that I wouldn't be the kid who got picked last.

I usually did get picked last, or at least that is how I seem to remember it. But here's the thing:

God is so big and so amazing and so freaking cool that not only did He pick us, but no one, not a single one of us got picked last.

Getting picked last on the playground (for me) was like losing the game before I even stepped out on the field. It didn't really matter if my team won or lost because I left the game knowing that I was the kid who was picked last. It occurred to me today that God wanted to make sure that none of us felt that way ever.

So why would I put a chapter like this in a book about dealing with mental health diagnosis? It's a good question, and it comes with a pretty simple answer. The process isn't just about taking medication or showing up to therapy, and it's not about talking to friends or even just working through things on your own.

It turns out that it's also about the spiritual, which can be the hardest part for someone like me to wrap my head around. You see, when you have lived your life with unstable relationships and you have questioned yourself at what seems like every turn, it can be challenging to think of God as your loving father who picked you when you wouldn't have even picked yourself.

So hopefully when you read this, you find that it really isn't so much about my story. I'm hoping that you see yourself a little or maybe a lot, but on this particular Sunday, I saw God who picked me because He loves me, and I saw God who didn't pick me last. And that, dear friend, isn't my story, but it is truly a story that belongs to all of us.

(The chapter above occurred on Sunday. I'm writing this paragraph the Tuesday after the chapter was written. You see, tonight I was driving home from work and talking to a dear friend of mine, and she brought up one more point that I think you might like to know. There is another verse in the Bible (Matt. 20:16) that says, "The First shall be last and the last shall be first." My friend clued me in on the fact that not only was I not picked last by God, but even though I may have been picked last on the playground, I was picked first as far as God was concerned. The same fact is also true for you! That turned out to be a pivotal thought for me, so I thought I would share it with you.)

12

Admitting It Is Half the Battle

That's the saying, isn't it? Admitting it is half the battle. I think the anonymous addiction groups say it as admitting you have a problem is the first step to recovery. Perhaps that's why when I addressed this for the first time, my therapist got so excited. I think the exact words used were "Praise the Lord."

The words that preceded that response from him were said by me. *"I am a lifelong abuse victim."* As I am writing this, I am sitting here staring at the worlds on this page, and it still doesn't make sense to me that those words would come out of my mouth.

My life is not what I expect abuse to look like. I had always pictured abuse victims as having black and blue splotches all over their bodies or a dossier of broken bones, sprains, and other injuries affiliated with altercations.

Yet somehow that is not what this looks like at all. And in the same breath, I have been held hostage by being forced to stay in a room and argue when all I want to do is leave so that I am safe from the mental and emotional abuse (caused by others and again and again by myself). I've been brainwashed (or I've brainwashed myself) to believe that things are my fault even when they aren't and believed an entire host of lies about myself that God's Word says isn't true.

I'm a victim of this thing that I didn't even know existed. It is this thing that was discovered long before there were boards of ethical conduct in medicine or activists from the ASPCA. It's something called learned helplessness.

Learned Helplessness is defined as a behavior in which an organism is forced to endure aversive, painful, or otherwise unpleasant stimuli and becomes unable or unwilling to avoid subsequent encounters with those stimuli, even if they are escapable.

I believe the term was first coined when these two psychologists started this study where they consistently exposed these animals to painful stimuli over and over. Eventually the animals gave up trying to escape the pain even when they could easily do so. They were used to it, and this pain became "normal" for them.

When I first found out about this, my immediate thought went to circus elephants. This isn't a painful example, but I remember at some point in life being told that baby circus elephants have this thick rope which is attached to their neck (collar-and-leash style). Try as they might, those baby circus elephants can't break the rope. And eventually they stop trying. Then when they stop trying, the elephant handlers start to decrease the thickness of the rope until it gets to the place where a thin rope can guide and control a huge, fully grown adult elephant.

Then if there is an event at a circus such as a fire and an elephant were panicked and snap that thin rope that tethers it, that elephant is no longer useful for purposes of being a circus elephant because now it knows (for the first time in the elephant's life) that it is stronger than the rope that holds it.

That example may not hold the qualities of painful stimuli, but I am rather certain it's the same principle. Learned helplessness—as the elephant has enough power to break the rope but just doesn't realize it because he or she has been conditioned to believe it's not true.

It sounds very freeing, doesn't it? To know this thing exists and that it's even a thing. It may even be empowering, and in a way, it is because now you know that you can recondition yourself to not believe the lies you have either been conditioned to or taught yourself to believe. However, here is another place where the psycho-therapeutic professionals should have some sort of warning meeting which would go something like this:

You are ready to make this proclamation, and you have worked hard to get here. You are more self-aware now than you have ever been. If you have become your own advocate, may you even hear. You've been honest and participated in the meds and the talk sessions and have shown up for the process a lot more than you haven't. But before you make this statement, that you are a victim of abuse and desire to be set free from that label, there are a few things you should know—almost like a list of side effects that may occur when you take your stand.

1. *Fear: You have been taught that history repeats itself, and the fear that you cannot break free can be strong.*
2. *Anger: You may be so angry at yourself or at others that it just out and out eats at you. This may not be part of who you are and may be something totally new to you, which makes it something you have to learn how to deal with.*
3. *Defeat: You may not win every battle you think you should, and you will have to learn that sometimes the win is just learning to walk away from a no-win situation.*
4. *Abandonment: The people who have always said that they loved you would be there for you and protect you may not. They may leave you or disapprove of the fact that you are now standing up for yourself, being your own advocate, and becoming a healthier human being.*

Believe it or not, that is just the start of the list. I am blessed to have a therapist who is prepping me well. Even with that blessing, I still have to read the Medication Stigmata chapter of this book every now and then. I keep saying this, but getting better doesn't always look like the thing that people expect, or at least none of this is what I thought it would be. The thing is that I've admitted it. So bring on the rest of the battle because no matter what comes my way as I am crossing the borderline, I know *God's got it*!

13

Okay, So Half the Battle May Have Been Overstating Things a Bit

It turns out those anonymous support groups are definitely on point when they say you have to admit to things. That is absolutely the first step, but it is exactly that—one step. Unfortunately for me, it wasn't a step that happened at the beginning or even the end of the journey. It was one step after a myriad of missteps—just one step in the middle. I'm sitting here tonight (which is about a week after I wrote the last chapter), and the realities of this book are hitting me hard. It's hard to imagine me finishing this project—quite possibly because I have never completed anything close to a project of this magnitude before.

One thing about this victim (me) is that I've been hiding it and covering it up for a long time. In part because I didn't realize it was true, but it had a lot more to do with the fact that those side effects, doubt, anger, fear, and abandonment—okay, not so much the anger but the rest of them—have been used as defense mechanisms, which is to say that I have been self-deprecating to keep myself from being disappointed. I am afraid of failure, and why wouldn't I be? As far as I am concerned, I've failed at everything I've tried to do (which may not be the most realistic perception of my life, but it's one that I've been clinging on to as if my life depended on it for longer than I can remember).

We work with the tools we are given. I'm not a betting person, nor am I a professional therapist or med doc. When you come right down to it, I'm nothing more or less than a layperson with nothing that qualifies me to tell my story, except the fact that I've made mistakes. So unless you count the fact that I have a story to tell—and by God's grace, I'm in a position right now to tell and hope that it helps others—you may not understand why I'm telling my story at all. What I want this book to do is just open the door to discussion and take the dark and twisted madness out of having issues with mental or emotional health.

So again I submit that we work with the tools that we are given. Making the statement that I am the victim of abuse doesn't stop the abuse. I can tell you firsthand that it's easier to take a physical hit than to be verbally abused. The thing is I became dependent on verbal and mental abuse (which I did to myself more frequently than anyone). Someone would help me out, and I would wait on the other side of the help. And on that other side of the help (for me) was usually something like having it being held over my head or holding it against me in a future argument. That's part of what I was used to.

There is also the back-handed compliment (which is really the exact same thing)—you know the one that tries to be nice but falls about a foot short: *"That's a nice outfit, it looks good on you. I'm just not a fan of stripes at all."*

I kept trying (and sometimes keep trying) to do things to please *everyone* or to protect people (or myself) from everyone, and neither one of those things ever work out well.

Remember the backpack theory? I had almost four decades of personal life lessons in there before I even learned there was a backpack. Then all of a sudden, I turn into the kid who can't find the homework, the kid who has worked on the assignment for weeks or months. It's the big paper, the one that is due at the end of the term.

Here I sit, on this couch or the floor (I find sitting on the floor back to the wall, both feet on the ground comforting), in my therapist's office rooting through this metaphorical backpack, trying to find the assignment I need and, at the same time, trying to get rid of all the stuff I studied but had the wrong answers too.

It feels like you need them. After all, you've depended on this homework for years. It turns out you do, but not for all the reasons you thought you did when you first started down the path of talk therapy.

Let's stick with this example; let's say I find this paper in my backpack on pleasing my friends and family that I wrote when I was—I don't know—let's say eight. Now I'm thirty-nine, and I never realized it. But I am going with the same answers to actual questions as an adult that I did as a child.

Before I started therapy, I wasn't looking for new answers or even checking the old ones to see if they are still true. When I really started to work the talk therapy process, I figured out there were a lot of assignments in my backpack that I learned and thought were absolute truth but were never true to begin with.

When I was a child, I was expected to tell the truth. I'll be the first to admit that didn't happen as often as it should. I'm not proud of that fact, and actually I carry a great deal of shame in the fact that it's only really been in the last ten years that I have become known for being a straight shooter.

Here's how things went down. As a child and a teen, I made an art form out of putting dirty clothes under the bed and in the closet and carrying Cs and Ds in school. The hamper was right across the hall, literally two steps from my bedroom door. I knew that eventually certain things would happen, some related to me and some related to the feelings and emotions of other people in my family. I did this because when the time came for the explosion, I wanted the blast to be directed at me (jumping on the landmine before it exploded).

So inevitably there would be two questions that were asked.

1. *How many times had I told you?*
2. *Why do you do this?*

At the time, I didn't know the answer. Now I do. I also know the reason that this happened. Sometimes it was self-perpetuating. Bad grades—usually a report card, midterm report, or parent teacher meeting—would set that off. I've spent my life hearing that I could do better and be better if only I applied myself. I can tell you that is absolutely true! I can also tell you for a fact that those statements are absolutely demeaning.

Now the clothes thing—that was another story. I didn't know the answers to the questions back then. I do now. As an adult, I figured out that when someone wasn't feeling good about him or herself, there would be an explosive emotional argument. I didn't want the blast to be directed at me (instead of someone else), so I developed the clothes thing.

Fear:

How on earth do I send that last paragraph to press? It's the truth, and there are people who will understand. But there are also people who *will not*. I will be judged for putting it to print, for admitting to being a liar, and (as ridiculous as this may seem) for *not* continuing to hide the truth. As I am typing this now, I remember hearing more than once, *"If you tell anyone about this, you need to make sure they know what you put us through and that you gave as good as you got."*

There are very few conversations in life that I can remember word for word but that. That is one them. Some of them come from other people—other quotes like *"I'm the scum of the earth."* That quote was all mine. No one told me; somehow I just knew it was true, even though it wasn't.

For me it's the fear of being alone, of losing those you love and knowing that they may never see the truth for what it really is and be trapped where they are.

The word cycle applies often to several facets of my life. It allegedly applied when I was misdiagnosed—so much so that I had to be told several times the bipolar label didn't apply to me. Keep in mind at the time, I was being medicated for it and had no less than three medical professionals telling me it did. However, it turns out that the word cycle still did. I can see that now as I look back, and they are called cycles for a reason. I think that's why history repeats itself, unless you study it and figure out how to change your actions and reactions. That's the only way to truly change who you are. That's what started this book and specifically this chapter, which I had hoped would have a nice neat ending to it. I was also hoping that I would like myself more by the end of the chapter than I did when I started out, which really isn't the case at the moment.

Actually right now, I don't think I have either of those things in me. Doubt and fear are all so overwhelming. In spite of that, I am still ready for the next step, and God has still got me. The fear of the unknown, the fear of leaving all of the abuse and unwinnable arguments—all that fear is causing me to have a hard time taking my hands (and my mind) off of the process and giving it to God.

Tonight everything in that last paragraph won't allow me to sleep and leaves me wondering what will happen when this book is published. Yes, sir! Admitting it was the first step—a new first step. But it turns out it's still a long journey from here, and I will have to stay and steady the course if I really want to cross the borderline.

14

I'm Not Ready Yet

As I sit down to write this chapter, I am afraid. This probably falls under one of my biggest fears of all. When someone reads this chapter, they will know one of my secrets—a big one and one that I don't really wear on my sleeve.

From time to time, I hit points when I'm ready to call the game, when I don't like myself, or when I feel like the planet would be better off without me. Right at that moment, when I decide to turtle because I'm not ready to be fixed.

I'm usually scared and frustrated and unsure of the next move, and most of the time, I haven't even identified what I am thinking or feeling. But even if I don't know what I'm dealing with, the one thing I know is *I am not ready yet.*

I've gotten pretty good over the years at putting up a front that causes people to think that I am dealing with everything just fine and don't really need any help at all, or at least I like to think that's what it looks like.

The reality is that due to that fact, or in spite of it, recently I've grown some solid relationships. That result of that from time to time is my friends noticing when I "drop off the radar" even if I don't send out that e-mail/text notification of intent to "turtle."

Frequently I don't even realize that I have gone into that self-imposed isolated state until I get an e-mail, or voicemail. Someone will stop me when I'm on the run and tell me I was kind of quiet today or they haven't gotten a phone call lately and ask me if I'm okay.

Then when I say, *"I'm fine"* or *"I'll be okay"* or *"It's almost over"* or one of the other myriad of things I say that to me are almost scripted responses, I get an answer like "I'm praying for you" or something in that general line. Normally this would help me, but when I turtle, I'm so deep into myself that it just feels like I've hit a brick wall. So at this point, I'm all tense because I know what's coming next.

After the initial answer comes—the "do you want to talk about it"—and if the answer is no, that person will go on and tell you something that you already know God's Word says.

Keep in mind that for purposes of this discussion, I'm not ready to be fixed yet. So you need to know that I mean no disrespect to anyone, but when you are starting out in what feels like a great tragedy or are beginning to feel some huge emotions, sometimes you just aren't ready for the fix. When it all comes down to it, if someone tries to fix me early on in the isolation cycle, I will rail against it. When I rail against it, I end up calling myself an idiot or something even more extreme.

You have to understand that I have spent a lot of time running from such things (like my own emotions and thoughts) because I was told by myself and others these were bad things. I frequently feel like I don't matter and like there are so many other things or people that are so much more important than I am. Now deep in my brain, I know that God has called me to be His kid, and He wants only good stuff for me as any father should for his children.

The thing is that in a moment like this one, I feel like I don't deserve any of it at all. In this moment when I pray, my prayers don't seem to come from the chick who knows she's Gods kid. I'm praying as the scared person who doesn't want to say the wrong thing and show the crack in the armor that makes it evident that I am so unsure of myself.

So I am actually praying that the actual person who I am talking to will just stop talking. This sounds counterintuitive, but that doesn't mean that I want to be alone; it just means that I don't want to deal with whatever is going on right at that moment.

When I'm in this place where I'm not ready to be fixed yet, the more uplifting or relevant the thing, the more I feel like an idiot. I've spent the better part of a lifetime overinflating things and being shifty and running from everyone and everything.

As a result, not only does it not feel like the amazing truths that are being said don't apply to me (even though they probably do), but now it also feels like I'm wasting time with the friend who I'm talking with.

Everyone is so busy, and the world is a dark and scary place. I try to be one who encourages by finding truth and good and calling it out. Today's things are in this day and age of phone calls and voicemail messages that rarely get returned unless you count e-mails, text messages, or Facebook messages.

How do you ask for help when you're ready without setting out alarms? See, my friends—they all have their own families, demanding jobs, and all the other things going on that I elevate as I demean my pathetic little life. Which is kind of ironic because as I sat here and typed that last paragraph, I realize that even on a good day, when I feel like I have it more together than not, I demean myself and don't place myself on equal footing with my friends and family.

(One of the things that I tend to get right rather consistently is making sure that all people are treated with love and respect, and come to think of it, I'm pretty good at jumping in and helping out when I can too.)

Yet to be totally transparent and shed light on the process—more often than not—the reason I'm not ready to be fixed can be for a number of reasons that include the following:

- It hurts too much to feel more than I feel right now.
- I'm afraid of what comes next.
- I don't know what to do next or how to respond to the person or situation standing right in front of me.

- I don't want to look past this moment because the next one could be worse
- Feeling lonely is good; I don't want to be fixed because I'm not done being angry and scared.
- I want people to think that I am fixed and don't see the hurt, fear, or anger that I am trying to hide.

There is more that could be added to this list but those are pretty good starting blocks! It's kind of crazy to think that this is who I am at this point, that the chick who has come far that she's writing the book still has something this basic to work out, but it's true.

God has me, and I know that. What I don't know is how to hand everything over to Him and leave it in his hands.

What I do know is that He is still working on me, and there is a lot of work done and even after I've finished crossing the borderline, there will still be a great deal of work to do because life will go on even on the other side of the borderline.

15

I Don't Want to Do This Anymore

There are these points in the talk therapy process where—to be candid—I just don't want to do it anymore. I'm sitting the seat of my car feeling like that right now.

I have a session tomorrow with my therapist, and I don't want to go. As much as I'd like to believe that I'm all better and don't need this anymore (which happens frequently when meds or life are working for me), I want to believe that I am looking for an escape hatch tomorrow. I'm not going to get the answers to my questions or, more likely, not the answers I want.

Here's the problem with going to an ethical (or, as my pastor put it, "real deal") therapist. It's been almost two weeks since my last session, and each day since that session has felt more debilitating than the one before it. The reality is that I have virtually gone radio silent and am trying to isolate myself, but it's not really helping at all.

At the time I am writing this book, I live in an environment where the attacks are personal, volatile, and designed to get you to hit back with words. The problem is that I am at a point in my life where I see the cycle and am doing my best to refuse to participate.

The other issue that constantly comes up is that you can't address an issue like this with someone who doesn't see that there is an issue at all. The more I am looking at this process, the more evident it becomes that this kind of confrontation rarely does anything short of the equivalent of either pouring gasoline on the fire or ripping open the existing wound.

The thing is no matter what lies are being told or what truth I'm being confronted with about my past, I respond by going back to being a sixteen-year-old kid, the one who is scared out of my mind and has lost the will to fight back. It's not that the will has been taken from me. I have to be candid here. As an adult, I was the one who gave it up, but now I just refuse to retaliate because it won't do anything but cause damage.

This is really one of those grown-up moments. The moment that you realize that there is more damage done by fighting a lie than there is trying to get someone who foundationally believes that lie to see the truth. If you ask the people who tell or accuse you of these lies, they will tell you that it's not a personal thing.

It turns out that that is a lie too. It's personal—very personal.

When I talk to my friends, they tell me it shouldn't matter and that these lies are Satan's way of trying to get victory over (and a foothold into) my life. I bucked that statement for a long time and then found out that they are right, and it's not just theoretical.

What I'm trying to do now is find a way to explain all this and the fact that someone saying something is not enough to make it true. Right now this is just one more level of pressure that I will have to learn to deal with until I get to the place where the hurtful words don't matter.

The thing is the attack that took place last week was an attack against some of the things that I work hard to do. I am not the person I used to be. So no matter how much I try to make the words not matter, letting them roll off of my back like water off a duck, there is this piece inside me that asks if I am still the girl I used to be.

So now I sit here, writing this and literally not wanting to go to therapy tomorrow. The irony is that based on what I think and what I've been told by people who know much more on the subject than I, there is much less work ahead of me than that which I have already done.

The question then becomes what is being all whole and healed worth to me.

Here's an example:

I used to be dishonest. Strike that. I was a liar, and at that time, I didn't realize I was. My perception of reality was skewed, and I believed or made up truths that at times were not even close to reality. This is something that I am ashamed of and wouldn't even put into this book except that I'm hoping it makes it easier for someone else to talk about it in the future or at least know they aren't alone, and they can overcome.

When I started making changes, I decided that one of the things that was high on my list was to become an honest person. I am continuing to work hard to make that happen. Did you know on TV how there is that three second delay for live broadcast? That infamous delay that is supposed to be enough time for TV sensors to push a button to black out (or bleep out) profanity, vulgarity, or unfit content that violates the standards of broadcasting,

My brain used to work a lot like that, only kind of in reverse. Let me explain. I tend to be a quick thinker—pretty fast on my feet which was kind of necessary back in the day, and I didn't realize that I was doing this at the time, but now I see that I would replay real time conversations in my head.

- This is so I can make sure that the response I give either lines up with other responses or
- To try to predict what someone was going to say or do next

The thing is that people didn't know what was going on. The responses that were coming out of my mouth on one level sounded crazy but on another level usually held just enough possibility that they might be true.

Here's the victory moment. I can *honestly and with 100 percent accuracy* say that I have given up the "tape delay" in my conversation.

I work hard to be honest and candid and tactful and direct. It's totally a conscious decision for me.

Last fall, there was an incident where I accidentally struck another vehicle while driving my car. The bulk of the details don't matter much to this chapter, so suffice it to say that I was on my way to work and the police were called.

I was at fault, and the officer wrote me a ticket. The truth is the peace officer who wrote me the citation told me that if everything was being taken care of by the insurance I could plead not guilty and the officer would not show up to the hearing and the citation would be dropped.

So then it became a debate between family and friends and myself. I was told this: "This is how the system works, and it's okay to plead not guilty even if you did what they said you did." The thing is I couldn't do it. I wanted to, and on the back end it, turns out that the citation carried three points for my driving record. My thing is if I'm really invested in the process of becoming the person that I am called to be. If I want to be a person who is honest, how do I say I didn't do something I did?

So I paid the fine, plead guilty to the traffic ticket, and took the tree points. If it comes up in conversations, I still hear "You should have just plead not guilty, that's how it works these days."

I don't want to do it. I don't want to be who I used to be, and I don't want to go to therapy tomorrow just to walk out of the appointment with more questions than I walked in with. Perhaps—just maybe—it'll prove that I'm willing to pay the price to get just a little bit closer to being all healed and complete. Maybe (just maybe) I'll be a better person for it too. I won't know until tomorrow, so I guess we'll just have to see what happens.

16

The Games I've Played

So this is one of the parts of this book where I get to call myself out on something I just did in the last chapter. The majority of this book was written over a couple of years, and there were very few chapters that I went back and read immediately after they were written. Most of the chapters just kind of sat there, waiting for me to come back and reread them and get them into an actual first draft form in the hopes that a publisher will read them and decide that it is worth putting them into an actual book.

This chapter isn't one of the prewritten ones. In the last chapter I said that I didn't want to go to that therapy session. That is a total head game I play with myself frequently. I say I don't want to go, and at the same time, I do. It's not like that very first session that I went to with my current therapist, the one where I was scared because I didn't know what I was getting into.

Now I say that I don't want to go (mostly to myself) because I know what I'm in for. I know that sometimes the process can take so much out of you that the one hour in the morning can just mess you up for the rest of the day, or it can even take a couple of days to feel like you are back on your feet again.

I know that things that I think I have fixed, the assignments that I have answered (in a way that I think is correct) and have put back in my backpack may have just been placed there to help me figure out that I have just answered more of the questions wrong again.

I don't want to be the person that I was, but if the therapy sessions are what I need to be the person that I was created to be, bring them on. That doesn't mean that I am not going to keep playing the "but I don't want to go" game in my head. I've not missed an appointment with this therapist because of it.

I just thought it was worth mentioning.

17

Why Me?

It's the middle of a night in September. Actually it's closer to Sunday morning than it is to Saturday night. September has become a powerful month in my life. I have a couple of anniversaries that aren't so easy to get through, there is the whole 9/11 thing, it's suicide prevention month, and there are other anniversary dates in September too.

It's harder than it probably should be. Facing the stigma of having at one time been suicidal and holding the memories of those you've loved and lives that have been lost to suicide. You've read about the fact that I am a victim of abuse but there is this other thing that I am now that I didn't used to be.

I'm a survivor. I equate it to things that it almost feels like I shouldn't because on several levels, they are not the same. Yet on many levels, they seem to parallel. Addiction and life-threatening illness seem so much bigger than my past and what I'm going through, which causes me to desire to minimize my life experiences.

The ironic thing is that it all leads to the same end. People die as a result of addiction and terminal illness every single day. People dealing with mental illness and physical, emotional, and mental abuse also take their life every day because of many (often unknown) reasons. Those who don't struggle with those thoughts or deal with those kinds of issues may never understand.

So to be transparent about it, there have been *several times* in my life that I have been left asking, why me? There have been times that this though has literally spared me from actually allowing myself to give in and commit the act of suicide, yet other times I have asked why couldn't I get to go like those who have ended their lives get to.

Knowing that this will go public makes it much harder to write this chapter, but in the same breath, this book would be worthless if I didn't include this too because it is real. You would think pulling out of the dark and twisted places and back up into the light was the end of the story, you know, that "happy ending" place where things get all happy and life becomes easier.

That's really not always the case. It's not like it's a black and white thing. There are definitely shades of gray. I've asked the question, "How do I know when I need help?" The answer is amazing in its simplicity. If you are asking yourself if you're safe, there is a good probability that you are.

It's when you stop asking that question that you may have crossed back over the line. The thing is when you stop asking the question … Well—and I can't speak for anyone but me here—in the moments when I stop asking the question, I tend to forget that there even is a line.

Remember being a kid? Taking a stick and drawing a line in the dirt, or rocks or laying the stick itself down and making a line then daring someone to cross it. For me the answer is kind of like that. You can see that line right up to the point where you step over it, but once you do you forget that it was ever there.

Maybe a better way to put it is if you can't see it, it's easier to pretend it wasn't there in the first place.

So why me anyway? That's the question. Why am I here, and why aren't they? I promise you it's not that I'm any better than anyone else. If you look back through history of famous people, you'll quickly see that intelligence has nothing to do with it, or perhaps it does. Brilliant men and women have lost their lives in this battle. It affects the wealthy and the destitute, men and women, young and old.

People that you don't think have a care in this world. People surrounded by those who love them and those who seem all alone or standoffish.

This is another one of those chapters that I wish had a gift wrapped ending, but it doesn't.

18

What's Fair? (I think It's that Thing that Happens on the County Fairground Once a Year with the Good Food and the Parade)

There's this one movie where a character wakes up every morning and forgets everything that has happened until the moment that the character wakes up.

There was a time when I thought life would be great if it were like that. If you lost all the hurt and the pain and abuse and abandonment. If every day you get a chance to hit the reset button and start over from scratch. It would be a life where people look out for you and keep you safe.

Now I know that is not what life is actually about. I possess qualities that I believe are good and wholesome because I've been treated poorly in the past. I've learned lessons from my own experiences. I've yes Ma'ammed a four-year-old little girl just to be told *"I'm not a ma'am, I'm a princess."* I don't hold all the secrets. If I did, the book would be much thicker and on the bestseller list right now even before it is published.

The thing is, right now, I am the sum total of what I have learned what I have achieved (good and bad) of my personal and spiritual beliefs. I am not finished. This is just one of the many chapters to be written not only in this book but in the story that is my life. Long after you close this book, the story will continue on.

Everything good and bad is a part of who I am. Some of the losses have been massive. I have not had nor do I now possess the tools to cope with all of the things life throws at me. It's not fair! *Ha.*

Fair—now that's a funny word. They have this street fair every year in this town called Ephrata, Pennsylvania. It's billed as the largest street fair in Pennsylvania, and I'm certain it is. It's more crowded with people every single year without fail.

Then there's the other fair we find ourselves longing for. The one that makes kids count out gummy bears to make sure that we all have an even number. It makes a friend of mine sort out smarties or any colored candy really, to make sure that all the colors are equally represented. It's what we believe happens when justice falls where we believe it should and is handed out in a fashion we agree with.

The thing is that kind of fair isn't life. It's not supposed to be, and it really never was. So when you take the fairness out of the equation, here is what you get. There is a stigma associated with emotional and mental imbalance. There aren't seven-year-olds running around saying, "When I grow up, I hope I need therapy." The reality is that there are diagnoses that carry larger stigmas and less understanding than others. Suicide will happen no matter how hard we fight for recognition, prevention, and awareness.

People will hurt and not realize that they are hurting, let alone how to ask for help or if it's okay to do so. They strike that *I* was (and at times am) embarrassed because I feel like I am not worthy and, at the same time, don't deserve to be the person that I am. I will feel like I am the worst person and, in the same breath, like I am not as bad as some other people out there.

I will feel loved without being loved and not always be able to recognize it when I really am. I will hate myself and feel like I need to experience the worst pain because of who I am and, in that same moment, want myself to stop hurting. I will want to cut myself so deep and so long that it would literally take my breath away but know the pain that I will leave in my wake if that were ever to happen.

I will surround myself with people I love and that are good to me when I am getting better and not know how to hold on when things get bad and hurt so much that I can't breathe for the crying. I will feel crazy even when I'm not, and now I will always remember what it was like to be trapped in an overmedicated misdiagnosis, having to fight with my whole brain to get past the slow reflexes and the night terrors and bad lessons I had packed away in my backpack.

This is just one more chapter and really doesn't change any of that at all. It does not heal the pain that comes from losing someone you love; it doesn't stop them from dying or leaving you behind to try to deal with what's left of a life that they helped you to start to put back together.

It doesn't stop me from having to admit to who I was. I was a liar who hid from the truth and manipulated people without thinking about it—slick as ice. I could push buttons like no one else on the planet. I was friendly but so alone. I would pull away I was scared and …

If had a magic wand, I would change my nature back then at its core, but the truth is that nothing I can do will make this woman in her twenties less angry and apprehensive about walking into therapy or being committed voluntarily or otherwise to any mental unit, hospital, or program for evaluation. It won't stop misdiagnosis or overmedication from occurring.

There are times when I can't even keep from calling myself an idiot the next time I react without thinking. My hopes for this book hasn't changed from the time you opened the front cover. I pray that instead of seeing a freak or a monster of someone who should have done better, someone who you may think "doesn't need the pills" even though they do help *a lot*! I hope you will see someone who is human and admits to the fact that I do need help even though I don't always recognize it or even know how to ask for it.

I think the truth for most of us who have carried or do carry the borderline personality disorder diagnosis realize that it's something that we may struggle with for a lifetime. I feel blessed (my friends call it lucky) to see it for what it is. I know that it doesn't have to be a life sentence, but that means that I have to keep putting in time and work and need to continue to do so if I want to keep making things better.

No one has all the answers, and it's hard. The process is hard for everyone, not just the patient. Families and friends can be affected by or cause much more dysfunction than most can imagine. These folks may never see it as dysfunction because it's always been the way it is, or perhaps it's less toxic than the generation before. It is hard to get out from under any pattern if you don't realize that it exists.

Then there are the friends who see a good person who suddenly flips the script for no reason at all going postal or AWOL or choosing to isolate. Then there is the therapist or med doc who can't get a good read because the story they are getting is so far from the truth or so inconsistent and not even remotely related to the real truth at all.

Medications can work, and when they do they're amazing; the clarity is amazing. There is nothing like being able to have one uninterrupted thought at a time and see it through till the end. When it happens, I lie in bed after taking that one little pill on top of my tongue and taste that orangey flavor, and the back of my brain wonders why I am still taking it because I feel fine. (If anyone asks you, the reason I still take the pill each night is so that I can continue to feel fine.)

My family doesn't understand because they can't see how important love and respect really are and how much it hurts to feel like you don't belong or deserve happiness and love.

My friends—at the moment, I was working hard to treat them fairly with love and respect. I have to tell you; I do still isolate when things get bad because, literally, I don't want to infect the happy people, and I don't want to hurt these amazing people who have poured good lessons and truth into my life.

This is where I really believe that the wisdom of God has affected everything. He's giving me friends who love me. I am friends with a pastor and his wife who—although they understand my dark and twisted moments better than most in any profession even if they don't always agree with my perspective—appreciate and get the fact that I chose to be honest even when things get scary. I have a therapist who acknowledges the fact that there is a connection between meds, the cognitive behavior therapy, and God. This guy doesn't try to make up an answer himself (which candidly cuts both ways sometimes). So even though the borderline keeps shifting and some days it's brighter than a newly painted line on the highway and others like a line drawn in the sand with a stick, I will keep crossing it and dancing around it and working to help people understand. Because in my journey and in this place of prayer and searching for understanding of and for myself, there's nothing left to but focus on crossing the borderline!

19

It Really Is as Scary as It Looks (aka Do Try This at Home)

I started typing this chapter out, got about halfway through, and ended up deleting it and starting over. I bring that up because finding the right angle to come at this chapter had been a bit tricky for me. I was reading a response from a friend on a chapter that I had leaked in a pre-first draft form when I suddenly realized how scary this has to be for those around the people who are affected with such things as depression, chemical imbalances affecting the brain (i.e., bipolar), personality disorders, and labels of mental illness or EDP (emotionally disturbed person).

It doesn't matter what you call it; it's not what is considered normal. I'm quite certain that on some level, it's a lot more common than we tend to think it is. There are four things I think everyone should consider when dealing with such matters.

1. There are two sides to every story (at least).
2. The person who is affected is likely in denial, embarrassed, ashamed, doesn't realize there is trouble, doesn't know how to deal with trouble, and doesn't know it's okay to ask for help because of one of the other things I just mentioned.

3. It is likely that there is perceived failure somewhere in the equation.
4. No one talks about it.

Right now, I think I am probably about 90 percent what I would call "fixed" and still at this point in time the hardest aspect of this for me can be the self-centered nature of the diagnosis and treatment process. This is complicated by the fact that the patient is rarely able to accurately recount events and honestly believes, in all sincerity, that we they are saying is true.

I can tell you that I sat down in front of countless doctors, nurses, therapists, one peace officer, and other trained professionals before I was actually to the place where I was ready to find the answers. Each one of them started with the same basic questions. "What has brought you here today?" And I, for the most part, never really told them why I was here. I would give them a symptom and expect them to decipher the clues.

Regular medical docs and surgeons have an advantage to some degree. If you walk into your primary care physician's office with a fever or a cough, at least you have a starting place. If you have a referral to a surgeon or a specialist, they have the advantage of having someone else having taken the first look.

I walk into my med doc's office and see the physician's assistant I usually see. My cough is the symptom I'm there for. As I'm talking with her, I cough; she then sees me blow my nose and comments on the interesting color of the mucus. Then we head over to the table, and I hop up and she listens to my heart and lungs. Next she looks into my eyes and nose and ears, and now she knows I have a sinus infection.

I didn't tell her I had a sinus infection; I just came in for a prescription for the "good" cough syrup that will definitely quiet the cough.

It's an actual phenomenon in medical practice. It occurs when the patient will sit through an exam or a fifty-minute therapy session and then, at the last possible second, asks his or her question or makes his or her statement that is more important than everything he or she addressed during the entire session or exam. You can look it up as "doorknob question" or "doorknob phenomenon."

I've had grandparents (more than one) pass away with some form of cancer. When I get a cough, there is always something in me wondering if it is more than a cough. So I started thinking. What if you are someone who is around someone dealing with an issue of mental and emotional health?

Here is what I would want to know if I were the person dealing with someone else who is in the shoes I wear:

1. *You'll likely want to blame them or fix them*: Unfortunately it almost never works that way. It's more probable that they will need help or solitude or maybe just time to figure out what the problem is and where it came from.
2. *Be quick to listen and slow to speak*: This comes from personal experience and is kind of tied into point one. However, when I started down this path, I didn't know where my issues came from. I thought it was all my fault and that everything that had gone wrong was all on me. After all, it was my actions and reactions that had brought me to where I am. Initially I heard frequently, "There is nothing wrong with your personality, and you don't need those pills." (Little did I know.) The thing is these statements, although well intentioned, made me feel more condemned and as a reaction I would cling to that wrong diagnosis as much as the right one.
3. *It's embarrassing and humiliating*: It shouldn't be, but it is. I realize now that as much as I was embarrassed to be a psych patient, it had to be even more embarrassing for my family who had to explain where I was or (probably more frequently) why I wasn't where I normally was. That fact is compounded by the fact that the patient usually doesn't want people knowing what is going on.

4. *No One talks about it!* If there were only one thing I could change for everyone out of this list, this would be the one. It's the not talking about things that jammed me up in the first place. I can say this now because it's where I am in my journey, and I know the real risk. Not talking about this can literally kill someone or their progress on many fronts. It will kill things like relationships, self-esteem, and yes, even cost lives.

This isn't something that gets fixed overnight or even over a week or a month. I wish there were a way that I could express the sheer frustration and humiliation that comes with a stay in the locked adult unit of a facility focused on the caring for patients with severe mental or emotional distress; it doesn't cure anything. Most of the time, it's not designed to be a cure all. It's designed to be a bandage—a quick fix (as opposed to the whole healing process). What it (per my experience) should do is literally get you back on your feet and give you the tools to go out into the world and find a treatment program that will help you develop the tools to live a "normal" and productive life.

The paragraph above isn't frequently understood by family and friends of those of us who have had to go through and aspect of this type of care. It doesn't matter if we are talking inpatient, intensive outpatient, partial-day programs, outpatient therapy, or even "just" medication compliance. For a friend or family member to say "I want you to get everything fixed this time, so we don't have to do this again" is actually counterproductive and, frankly, rather unrealistic. It sets one more unobtainable goal for the patient and creates a level of frustration for them as well. See, I knew I was going to fail; at least that was how I felt. I set those goals for myself every time, and the first question I got when I was out or done or medicated was "do you feel better now?"**

Much like this book, everything changes so quickly, and just like life when those doors to the locked unit close behind you, it's like the turning of this page. It will lead you right to the next chapter in life.

**Now there are situations where long-term mental care is absolutely necessary. Based on what I've seen, what determines if that kind of long-term care is required is a combination of determining if someone can stay safe or keep others safe, the level on which they can function, and the patient's perception of reality. There are people who need long-term care, but that's not the case for everyone.

20

The Madness Within

This was so much easier when it was a medical diagnosis of a chemical imbalance. It's the dealing with the reality of the fact that a good portion of all of this is learned behaviors and programmed responses that there is no test to definitely determine who is diagnosed. That makes the whole thing much harder to deal with.

I had a bad day yesterday. It was long, and I was tired. I got my nails done after work which was supposed to be a *me* time. You know, that decadent time when you just get to relax and have the world revolve around you for an hour or so. The thing is the place where I get my manicures done is about an hour away, and usually I love the drive to and from. But on this particular day, something happened. From the time I left work to the time I got to the spa, I was mad. Not just regular angry but downright mad. Then by the time I got home, my mind and my emotions were a raging ball of fire.

This wasn't the norm for me. At least it didn't feel like it is. However, I also knew that I had never been as aware of what was going on with my emotions as I was last night. It's something that I think may be a leftover byproduct of abuse or living in a dysfunctional environment, but even I have to admit that this is its own brand of crazy.

This is the kind of madness when anyone can say anything, and it will go wrong. I can walk into a room and hear "Hi, how did your day go?" And the response that I want to give is *"My day was fine! Why do you always have to interrogate me!"*

For me, on this particular night, everything was complicated by the fact that this madness was all that I was capable of feeling. So at least I could minimize the damage. I went to my room and tried to escape and be left alone and mellow out. I grabbed my computer, sat down, and finally got a few minutes of silence. In less than thirty seconds from the time I sat down, my cell phone rang. "I need your help with …" I can give you the rest of the sentence, but it doesn't really matter. All I needed at this point was to be left alone for the night. I was angry, and I was hurting and I was feeling so alone, and as far as I was concerned, there was no one who would understand how I felt. Even if they would, I wouldn't be able to acknowledge it. I got off the phone and somehow got the person who needed "immediate" assistance to wait until morning. Then someone else tagged me on the computer and wouldn't let me go even though I'd stated that this wasn't the best night for a conversation. Now I was just totally seeing red and couldn't handle things anymore.

I was actually way past the point of crisis now, and I didn't take my pill because I didn't want to sleep (I wasn't on the antidepressant yet). (The way I saw it, I didn't deserve it, and it would probably only cause nightmares anyway.) I was angry and combative and then it happened. All of a sudden, there was someone at my door. "Come out here and look at this when you get a minute."

Not "Are you busy?" or "What are you doing?" but "Drop everything and come here." Then it turned into "Since you are here anyway, can you just send this tonight?"

Forget the fact that (even though I hadn't told the person I was helping) I'd put someone on hold who refused to respect the fact that I needed to be left alone (when in my defense, I gave them fair warning) in the first place, and they were now on the computer, waiting for my return. Forget the fact that I was hurting so bad emotionally that even cutting myself wouldn't bring any kind of temporary relief right now, and forget the fact that I was feeling alone and defective and like a monster. I was fully aware of how self-centered and irrational I was being and in that moment. I couldn't find any tools that would allow me to stop this, let alone reverse it. Now I got to deal with an e-mail carrier that I had been begging someone to change from for more than ten years and a web-based sending program that literally took thirty minutes to upload and send an attachment that would normally take less than five minutes with any other e-mail carrier.

It felt, at this point, like I'd brought all this on myself, but I was not sure how. It really still feels like it's all my fault but I don't know when the change took place. I know when I left work, I was kind and respectful gal, and by the time I finally took my pill (six hours after the normal administration time), I was totally out of control and left with less than three hours to sleep.

I'm sitting here now typing this and I realize how crazy it all sounds. If you haven't lived through it or lived with someone who has this kind of thing kick in on them, you may not understand. I'm sitting here right now and I'm not far enough away from the incident to even know what it was that set me off.

I do know this needs to be a part of this book. I know that my responses have to do with being broken and not having the right answers. In your backpack, you need to deal with the things you come up against every day. Outside of that, I can't tell you much.

What I can tell you is I'm sending this beginning of a chapter in rough draft form to my therapist and will finish it up in a couple of weeks. I'm hoping I'll have more to add to it. I'll be back then.

I haven't had session yet, but hindsight is 20-20, and you know how all that goes. Writing about it now feels like a switch was flipped. There had to be something that sparked the anger, but I still don't know what it was. It's that kind of heat that would have driven me to spend some time in the locked mental unit. To be transparent, it scares me that I didn't ask for help that night; someone could have gotten hurt!

It's embarrassing and shameful to me that even now, as I'm sitting here typing this passage for a book that I hope to have published, I know that day "out of nowhere" comes this anger and hate and hurt. I don't know how to describe the pain. I didn't cut, I didn't want to, and it wouldn't have helped if I did. The pain was just too deep and too severe, and it's brought me to tears to just type this much tonight (meaning the last two paragraphs).

How do you go to someone you respect and seek counsel from and say I can't turn off the anger and the hate, knowing anything they say will only make things worse? All right, I say make things work, but the honest truth is anything they say is unlikely to be heard and more likely to be met with bad reactions, anger, and denial.

I'll figure it out; I'm sure. But for now, on to the next chapter.

21

Leaving the Past in the Past (The PTSD Chapter)

Last month marked the end of the second year I've spent working with this therapist. He is really good at what he does, and it's been a two-year process of what turns out to be a great deal of positive growth for me. So here we go, beginning year number three. This is the beginning of the first year that I am truly properly medicated (outside of something little for anxiety or something to help me sleep) with Remeron. This means that there is a lot to talk about right now as far as how things have changed. It's kind of its own can of worms being on medication I mean. In the metaphorical can with the dirt is now all of this new stuff I didn't know to expect, or maybe a better way to say it is that I didn't plan on it. If you read the Medication Stigmata chapter, you might think it were only roses growing in the dirt but not so much.

Actually there are plenty of holes and excrement being put in with the dirt and the mud. This journey to get to be the person I hope to become is even trickier than I thought it would be. I know that's a goal that I may never achieve, but somehow, I do think I'm getting closer to having more days where the borderline is fading behind me as something I've crossed than the days that I feel the borderline creeping back up and nipping at my heels.

Since we are talking about the setbacks that have arisen for me, now that I am properly medicated; I am talking more about how I have never had any memories of growing up or being an adult for that matter. Not the same way I perceive that other people do. I have mile markers in my life (major events such as births, deaths, marriage, divorce, and other accomplishments or failures of myself or others such as I graduated high school in 1992), and I sort of know where things fit in between them. But I don't know that I've ever just remembered an event. Shoot! I haven't even had memories triggered by a smell or a song.

(I can recall details of an event without recalling the event or how I felt while the event was going on.)

Now that I am properly medicated, I am starting to get things back in bits and pieces. I wasn't expecting this to happen. So now that I'm getting things back, I have things to deal with that I have never had to deal with before. I was sitting in a therapy session, and I heard myself saying in my own, rather snarky, way, "There is nothing in my backpack that is even close to anything that would allow me to deal with such a thing."

This was one of those times that the only way for me to describe that statement now is *drama*. I'm so blessed to have a therapist who gets the dark and twisted and drama moments (even though I don't have a lot of the drama stuff going on).

I wish I could sit here and tell you that I have a formula or an answer that will work for everyone in every situation. I would love to be able to tell you that I have dealt with all the issues that have come up in my own past and put it all behind me as I move forward.

Unfortunately, life just doesn't work like that. Part of my dealing with all this is figuring out how to convey to you after the fact the pitfalls that happen during the process. This part—the PTSD part that comes from dealing with everyone and everything that happens in life both good and bad.

- ❖ Hiding the stuff from myself that I don't want to deal with
- ❖ Hiding how I feel about everything from anyone I know

- ❖ Trying to pretend that things are normal when they aren't, and I know it
- ❖ Automatic reactions to things that cause me to react (in a way) to things that I can't remember
- ❖ Having a déjà vu feeling and not being able to remember why it feels so familiar
- ❖ Being hateful, angry, sad, mad, scared, alone, and not being able to remember why
- ❖ Trying to figure out how to deal with the emotions of others (i.e., jealousy, anger, etc.) without taking them on and feeling responsible for them.

This process is complicated for me by the fact that I'm now lonelier than ever because where as I used to have six thoughts at once, the Remeron has really calmed that down. I hate to admit it, but it really is the right med for me.

So for now, I just keep dealing with all this to the best of my ability. It turns out that journaling (and the writing of this book) have been helping me a great deal. Talking about and becoming an advocate for removing the stigma from talking about issues of mental and emotional health and suicide awareness helps too.

With this being said, I'll just keep moving forward and continue the journey toward crossing the borderline.

22

Oh, Be Careful, Little Mouth, What You Say

There is this song that we used to sing as children in kids' church (which I'm not really sure, but for some reason, I think they called it junior church back then). Anyway, it goes like this:

> Oh, be careful, little mouth, what you say
> Oh, be careful, little mouth, what you say
> For the Father up above is looking down in love
> Oh, be careful little mouth what you say

It was actually a rather all-encompassing song that included the eyes, and ears, and if there were more, I forget the rest of it.

The thing for me as I randomly began to think about that song is that as life would have it, it is really very sound advice. On one hand, we are supposed to keep our mind focused on good things and stay positive, and on the other hand (as if they were clasped together with fingers interlocked) there is this term left in my brain from the nineties of GIGO (garbage in, garbage out). In computer terms, that means that your computer is only as good as the programming that is in it. When it comes to people, it's a little different but not so much really.

To me, the garbage in garbage out principle as it affects people—I'm trying to find the right words to express this. Let me put it this way; if I spend all of my time watching TV or movies that sensationalize crime of killing or violence or lies, I will become desensitized to these things over time.

Right now for me, there are things that are very huge on my "never wanting to do that again" list. We'll call it the antibucket list. Lying and manipulating people so that they do what I want them to do are two items that carry what may be the highest priority on that list. If I listen to music or watch TV that says it's okay to do those things, it would make it that much easier to slide back down that slippery slope.

Let me give you a totally different example. I was sitting in a meeting (actually it was a volunteer event) with someone who worked within the public school system, and the conversation turned to reference a student who had graduated years ago. The only person in the room who knew who this student was the person who was speaking. No one else in the room had ever met or even heard of the student. The conversations turned to people taking responsibility for their own actions. One person said, "It's like they are still a teenager." Someone else exclaimed, "Like they've never even grown up." Someone else said, "I hate when people are like that. If you are an adult, you should act like an adult."

I was sitting in this room (and was having an emotionally rough day even before this conversation even started), and I was now wanting to scream out. *You don't understand! You don't know what it's like! How can you be so judgmental when you don't understand what is happening in this person's life!*

The thing is that I didn't scream out or even comment. I know how insane it would be to do so. If this were a different time or place, I might make a statement. This isn't the kind of situation where what I have to say would be heard. Ironically if this same conversation went on a few years ago, the first thing it would have triggered would be me going to my internal place of self-loathing and hatred and would have caused me to want to hurt myself

So this might be a good time to put a few things out in the open. It also may be a good time to say that these are the notes of a woman on a journey of mental health. I'm not a med doc or a therapist or counselor or anything that has any kind of credentials that make me anything more than a patient and a life student in this field. There are many theories on what causes this kind of behavior.

It can be a really simple answer. If parents, role models, authority figures were examples of this type of behavior, and this is consistently what you see, then you may just be doing what you were shown because it's comfortable. It's what you know because those who have introduced the behavior to you were supposed to be the people you could count on to learn major life lessons from, and as a result, you may think it's how life is supposed to be.

Another train of thought is (and I didn't know this until it was explained to me by someone who knows much more than I do) if you have traumatic events in your life, you can stop emotionally maturing. When I started the last round of therapy (a little more than two years ago), it was suggested that my emotional age was between eight and ten years old.

What I know now, and what I bucked against that day, is the fact that the assessment was totally on target. I have to admit that a lot has happened to change that in the past two years, and being aware of a problem can really be a catalyst for change if you want it to be.

So here's the other item I'd like to say and the reason for the title of the chapter. You never know who is sitting in a room. You have no idea what they have been through or what life experiences have brought them to where they are or how anyone is going to take any given conversation. I am the first one to know how hard it is to understand. Right now, I live in a community that has deep roots in Germany and a part of my ancestry comes from Poland. Both of these communities per my experience are filled with what I could call a humble pride. These are the places I come from and live in. Showing weakness isn't something commonly accepted there or—let's be real—in the world today. That being said, there is a strong work ethic and a deep sense of taking care of things yourself that come from these communities too.

So here goes. We don't know any better, or at least I didn't. Well, I thought maybe life shouldn't have to be this hard. I knew that my life wasn't the way life is supposed to be. I would not have been able to tell you why or how. I knew I should feel like more than a child and should take more responsibility for my actions and myself.

The thing is I didn't know what it was supposed to be like. I couldn't have explained how I was any different from anyone else. I couldn't have told you that my responses and actions and reactions were all based on things that I had learned over the years or that they were designed (by me) to protect me in ways I didn't understand. Most of all, I didn't realize that the very same action and reactions were causing me more harm than good and were causing me to stay where I was and not grow as a person.

As a teen, I would make up stories knowing that they were not the truth but believing they were. I believed them and stood behind my beliefs, even when it meant defending them to my own detriment because I had filtered out the truth.

The list goes on from there. It's hard for someone who hasn't experienced it to understand it and even harder for those who have to live with someone or are friends with someone who has and is going through it.

It would be a lie of omission if I didn't tell you that for a long time, I didn't even want to fix the stuff that was broken. I knew that it wasn't "normal." I was pretty sure that I wasn't like everyone else. In my late twenties and thirties, I was someone who intermittently cut herself, and even that I didn't do like a "normal" person.

So what we say is important. Even if it's not about the person we are talking to, we don't know how it will affect them. Making a statement like "I wish they would just grow up" or "They don't even act like they are an adult" can have life altering consequences for someone like me. If I were in a different time and place in my life it could have sent me to a locked unit. Then I would have made up some lie about why I was really there—something that didn't involve me admitting that I didn't feel like I was a grown up when I was well over the age of eighteen.

Now I've told my story to you. If we're lucky, you'll be able to talk to someone else about it. That's how things change—one person at a time telling one story at a time and then relating it to someone else. That's the only way that people are ever able to cross their own borderlines or put an end to stigmas.

23

The Double Bind

It's really appropriate that this chapter come after Be Careful, Little Mouth, What You Say. To me it's interesting that after the majority of this book is written, there are still chapters like this one that I have to complete because I'm not finished yet.

This is not just to say that I'm not finished with book yet; actually at this moment in time, this book is not even on the list of things that I think I have come close to completing. What I should have said is that I'm nowhere near finished with the process of making sure that my mental and emotional health is good even after I've crossed the borderline.

There are certain events that evoke strong emotions in me in part because of my life experiences and in greater part because of my passion that people learn from my mistakes and ignorant decisions. I'm in the middle of my own double bind right now, and in its own way, writing this chapter is its own double bind that I will save for another time. I've already gotten ahead of myself.

Let's start with the basics:

Double bind—it's a psych term which the dictionary defines as "a situation in which a person is given conflicting cues, especially by a parent, such that to obey one cue is to disobey the other."

It says a parent but since I've found out what the term means, I've seen it happen in home, work, and friendship environments. This is a great time to remind you that I am not a mental health professional. I am just a gal who knows that things like the double bind don't get talked about and stay hidden for decades and make you feel trapped, like you are responsible for an outcome over which you alone have little or no control over.

This has all been rather vague, so let me give you an example. Let's say a child gets caught breaking curfew and he or she is drunk when he or she is caught. The parent or guardian starts to lecture him or her and asks a question like, "How many times have I told you?" The teen starts to answer and is met with the words "Don't interrupt me when I'm talking to you!" The lecture continues and the teen is asked another question. The teen remains silent because of what happened the last time the teen tried to answer. This time, the teen hears "Answer me when I'm talking to you!"

I'm forty-one years old as I write this, and as I am learning and growing, I am starting to see the double binds before they occur. I know this kind of flies in the face of my being relieved about being off tape delay and no longer trying to predict conversations before they occur. However, last night, the ability to see the double bind before walking into it saved me a great conflict.

I am a passionate person with strong emotions, and sometimes they jam me up and make it harder for me to deal with people on a level that everyone is comfortable with. There are three things that I am most passionate about: God and spirituality (not so much religion and there is a big difference.), family and friends, and shining the light on issues of mental and emotional health.

A situation occurred last night that combined two of those items (friends and mental/emotional health issues). I was worked up; I was all sad, mad, and hurting. It's me; it's who I am. You can call me weak, but I don't really think that's the case. So I told someone what was going on, and I have to admit that I kept things together a lot better than I thought I would in that moment. Then I went off on my own to deal and regroup and try to become someone who I would want to be around again. I did that rather quickly and went out to "rejoin society" and mostly to talk about anything other than the issue at hand. I didn't have a topic in mind, so I just went and sat and waited. And the person I told made a comment about how tender my heart was and how that was a good thing, but it just really seemed like I wanted to belong somewhere other than where I was talking with the person I was talking to.

There were years, decades of conversations, actions, reactions, and scenarios that led up to that moment, but anything I said would have landed me in the doghouse or worse. Today I am so angry with myself because I thought I was past all of this. I never dreamed that I would have the feelings and emotions that came from the situation.

Right now I am facing three scenarios:

1. Do or say nothing—let that person believe they are right
   - After all, the issue is theirs and not mine. I never said, dreamed, or imagined that what that person said was true.
2. Say that it's not true
   - By doing so, I am suddenly on the defensive and trying to prove a negative and that doesn't ever go well. If you don't believe me, just try to prove to me that you did not own a rhinoceros.
3. Say it's true
   - Which really isn't an option because that would be a total lie, and I'm not that chick anymore.

The thing is no matter how I feel or what I say, this is a situation that doesn't get better. This is a situation that I can't control or fix or put the brakes on. It just has to play out, and I have to pray for the best. I know God's got it, but right now, I'm just angry, hurt, dealing with a loss, and don't feel like I can talk to my friends about it—who are having to deal with the issue at hand on a totally different, and more intense, level than I do.

Perhaps in the next book, I'll have a better end to this chapter. But for now, at least the conversation on the double bind has been started again—after the borderline has been crossed.

24

Programmed Responses

For the most part these days, I do okay. I have my moments when I break, but I'm finding out more and more that these emotional breaks are not good indicators of my personal situation or my effectiveness as a person.

You see, everyone has their moments. Some are dark, lonely, or even angry, but no matter how good we are feeling, we all have our times when we are running in our own circle of doom. I keep going back to that paper that was once taped to the monitor in a friend's office. "My feelings are not the best judge of my effectiveness!"

I thank God for that. Let's face it; life really does move fast. It's so easy to get caught up in the moment and go back to the reflex responses. There is this thing that happens in my environment with great consistency. You get into the double bind I referenced in the last chapter and then you (or more specifically I) shut down. This means that I just stop talking because at this point, any answer I come up with will be not only the wrong answer, but it will also dig a deeper hole. So at that point, I just clam up.

Then as predictable as the most precision timepiece, the party who is looking to win the battle will say, "So now you're not talking to me?" Here's the issue. The phrasing has variations like "You aren't going to talk to me?" It doesn't really matter how it is said; the outcome is the same.

It changes the conversation. Those words can make me lock up tighter than a high security prison cell. I can really only tell my side of the story at this point because here is where I start to block out the conversation. I start to have panic attacks which for me will almost always inevitably lead to GI upset (the graphic details I will spare you). I can tell you that my programmed response has become "So what do you want me to say?!?!?!?!?!?!?!?!"

The reason for the exclamation point at the end of this is that I know that there is no magic working that will break the bind at this point.

So what do you do? How do you get yours out of the thing that has tangled you up for the better part of 40 years? *Pause.*

This seems like a good point to go back to discussing what rock bottom looks like because I am at that point where I am seeing how bad things are, and I know that they won't get any better unless you (and by you, I mean me) see a change that needs to be made. *Unpause.*

So I ask again, what do you do? Well you have a couple of options. First you can open your backpack and pull out the responses that you have been programmed (by yourself and by others) to give. At this point, for me, one of those responses tends to be "What do you want me to say?"

(I should tell you it wasn't always that way. There was a time when I would have responded and chosen to hit back with words. That's what I knew, it's what I saw, and I now see how wrong that option is.)

The thing is that by this point in the conversation, there is transparently nothing left to win on either side. That response usually means that I have been hurt or humiliated or both and am almost always very sure that I have little self-worth by this point. I am also sure that I am wrong and it doesn't really matter much if that is the truth to God or anyone else because in the moment, my believing it is enough to make it so for me.

So once that response is out there, fear begins to drive the conversation at this point, and believe it or not, for me that is a safe and secure place. I can't find the words to explain the fear to you, but even as I type this, my adrenaline is surging, my neck is tight, and I'm not even worked up over anything at this moment.

The fear is a huge part of it, but (as much as I hate to admit it, and I do) there is great comfort in the argument as well as certainty and consistency. You know what is going to happen, and you know there is going to be an explosion and release of all of the pressure at least of the moment. The tension may be over at this point depending on whom the exchange is taking place, or it could last a few more days. It's actually almost kind of predictable what the outcome will be depending on with whom the exchange is with.

Here's the thing. I have learned that I have to do better now as—an adult who is now trying to repack my backpack and redo assignments that were done properly for the past. Those same answers are no longer relevant to the things that I am now learning and who I want to be. For the most part, I am doing better, but when a bone breaks, it happens in an instant and takes weeks or months to heal. This broke over a lifetime, so it won't get fixed in a day. Remembering that fact always helps me to do better and feel better about myself.

25

Be Busy Being You

There is this movie that I love to watch and have ever since its release in theaters. There is this line in it where one character tells another that they are so busy being who they are that they don't even see how unique, remarkable, amazing, and outstanding they actually are.

I have to be candid. I probably watched the movie at least fifty times before that line jumped out at me. Today it did. This is after the majority of the book has been written. The borderline has already been crossed, yet I have to admit that yesterday, for reasons I could have controlled (but felt like I couldn't), I absolutely hated myself on several levels.

I felt like I disappointed myself, others that I care about, and most of all God. The only thing that kept me going was that God and a few of my friends believed in me and loved me more than I was capable of that day!

To me, I was just really weak and pathetic. To me, it sounded and felt like everything is failing, and all was lost.

The thing is the gal I am now—I like her most of the time and even on days when I hate me. I like me much more than I did back in the day.

It's this balancing act that's never ending. How do I be me and care for the needs of others without letting those needs overwhelm me?

In the movie, the character that is so busy being him or herself feels like an explosion waiting to happen, which is how I still feel more often that I'd like to admit.

I know that if I stop being me, if I go back to being manipulating, lying, and cheating myself out of everything that God has for me, if I try to be someone I'm not, if I … if I keep iffing, I lose who I am.

This is the first time that I have really figured out that in order to like who I am, I have to be me. In order to achieve my potential, I need to stop trying to be everything to everyone. It's okay to prioritize; it's okay to not say yes to everything that comes along. Believe it or not (and if you've read any part of this book I'm sure you'll believe it) the hard part comes when we or I have to ask for help.

I can't do everything and still be me. I've finished crossed the borderline, yet every time I turn around, there are new goals to be conquered. I guess the only thing left to do is to get busy being me because I'm pretty sure God isn't going to make another one.

Here's a tip for you if you're struggling to like yourself, and it's one that's been a big help to me over the last several years. Find yourself a few friends who you know are absolutely 100 percent honest with you all the time. Not the kind that are cruel but the kind of friend who will tell you the truth in love even when it hurts. Then become the kind of person that they can depend on and believe in. Then in those moments, when you just can't believe in yourself, you can know that they believe in you.

In the moments when I can't believe in myself, don't trust myself to make good decisions, or don't like myself much, I will think of my best friend and the fact that she loves me and believes in me and that she wouldn't lie to me. When I don't feel like I can trust myself, I still feel like I can trust her. So I trust her, and there are days when I must repeat that to myself at least fifty times through the day. "She believes that I am a good person with good values who does good things."

There was this one day when my therapist wrote on a piece of paper that I have normal responses to normal situations. When I have days where I feel like I am overinflating the situations that happen in life, I go back to the fact that I trust his assessment of me, and that can help bring me through.

26

Adrenaline Crush

There is this thing that can happen to trauma victims. When the body feels stress it can release this chemical called adrenaline. If the trauma that is experienced is severe such as broken bones, open wounds, or even things that would normally be catastrophic, suddenly the body can surge with this adrenaline. This will keep the body going even when it would normally give in to the injury or succumb to the pain and trauma.

As long as the body continues this response to the event with adrenaline, it causes superhuman reactions. This is the thing that allows little elderly frail grandmas and grandpas to lift the bumper of a car to save a child. What you may not know is that when the body senses that dangerous situation is over, the production of this chemical stops. Then it happens all at once. The body first starts to relax, then suddenly the hurt and ache and every pain and reaction that the body should have experienced (over an extended period of time) suddenly all happen at once.

I was a cutter or am a cutter, depending on how you look at it. I'm at this moment not sure that that impulse will ever go away completely. The thing is, for a lot of years, I was in a lot of psychological pain that I didn't talk about. I was embarrassed and ashamed, and it was something that I hid—and not very well. During a large portion of the time this was going on, I was manipulative and felt very alone because I refused to let myself get close to anyone.

It was this consistent pain. When you are in the hospital for physical pain, they always ask you for your pain level, with one being next to nothing and ten being the most intense pain anyone has ever felt. Emotionally on that scale, for *decades*, I was living my life at an eight or higher. I actually learned the concept of cutting while I was in the locked adult unit. When you cut your own skin, not real deep, not to do harm, but just to cause some pain and release some adrenaline, the adrenaline would change the pain from something that is just in my head (psychological pain) to something (physical) real.

As I understand it, what it came to be for me was quite different than it is for most. So you can't take the account of how I did this to be the norm. It became very ritualistic, very antiseptic, which could have had a lot to do with my medical training.

It doesn't much matter what a specific routine looks like or what leads up to it. What happens afterward is about the same for anyone who cuts, I think. We hide the wounds (which turn into scars) when we are in the throes of cutting. For me, it was pretty easy. At first, I try a few different locations across my body, but in the end, I found that the easiest place to not only cut but to hide the cuts and scars (being left handed) was my right bicep. It was easily hidden by longer baggy sleeves.

Over the past few weeks, I've been going through this emotional trauma. Friends that I thought loved and supported me, people that I counted on and trusted to give me good godly counsel have proven to not be who they represented themselves to be. I've lost a relationship that I depended on. It's been event after event after event, and I have been running on psychological adrenaline for weeks. Last night, that adrenaline left, and I crashed and was crushed—hard.

I thought I was doing so well and had it all together. I was doing my best to help someone else who was so much more effected by the situation than I was. When the adrenaline left and intense sadness and despair came over me—that's not even true—*I was angry at myself!*

Actually, even using the term angry is pushing the borders of the truth. I was cruel to myself with the words I was using. I'm embarrassed to tell you, but any judge in America would call the words I was using in my head toward myself as hate speech.

Up until this point, I "had it all together." I had control, and good things were happening, then eventually, when I was physically exhausted, it all came to a stop.

I don't' know if there is an actual term for it, but adrenaline crush seems like a good choice to me. I wouldn't even have brought it up if it weren't for this one thing. My reactions were my ways of backing up closer to the borderline that I have already crossed. It was me going back to the familiar place of blaming myself for "not seeing that coming" when there was no way that I could have even guessed what was headed my way. Believe it or not, it was actually more comfortable for me than dealing with the loss of friends and trying to help another friend who was hurting.

I didn't stay there; I gave myself some time and then put on my big girl boots and got back to where I needed to be. As much I'd like to say I didn't falter, I did. It's very likely that will happen again, but knowing what I know now will help me to eventually stop reacting the way that I did and help me act with thought and direction and move forward.

27

Who Moved Last?

I remember being a kid and playing board games with my sister on the living room floor with the TV on. I was a child of short attention span who didn't always do the best at multitasking and was inevitably left asking the question, "Who moved last?"

This morning, I am reminded of that question in a very different context. I've just come through what may be the darkest, most twisted four consecutive weeks of my life. I realize now that what I thought to be just a rough patch was much worse than I noticed while I was in the deep darkness of my own emotions and mindset.

I do this thing where I "turtle," and it starts with me sending out e-mails and text messages that basically state that things are on the rough side of life, and I am going what I term as "radio silent" but not to worry if I need help, I'll ask for it. Over the last few years, I've done that rather successfully and when the time comes for me to come out of my shell, I come back, and that is the end of the rough patch. And things go back to the status quo.

The thing is, this time that wasn't the case. Things went dark quickly, and I couldn't pull up or get myself out of the funk. Then two weeks later, there was another life event that caused me to go deeper. By the end of this four-week period, it was so bad that I was actively trying to figure out how to make a plan to end my life. The only reason I didn't go through with it was because I couldn't find a way that guaranteed me an easy exit without guaranteeing that someone would have to come after me and clean up the mess.

I'm someone who works very hard to expose this process for what it is. I'm trying to help educate and take some of the fear and the stigma out of the process. So there is not much that I hide as far as my emotions and my current state of mental health goes. Yet somehow, when it comes to the whole issue of being suicidal, there is so deep a stigma attached to it that it's hard to not at least want to hide the truth.

From an insider's perspective, it is any one or a combination of the following:

- Depression
- Defeat
- Anger
- Fear
- Low self-esteem
- Feeling like you've failed yourself or others (and *feel* is the word because it can often just be perceived failure)
- Feeling overwhelmed
- Frustration
- Self-loathing

The list goes on from there. When I hear others talk about it who have not been there, what I hear is that it is a sign of weakness. Personally I've dealt with people who don't understand saying things like you have to know that you are "worth more" or "a good person" and "really good at the things you do."

Life is a work in progress, and now I am trying to learn from my mistakes and do pretty good at that sometimes and not so well at it in other moments. I think this last time I turtled, the reason I didn't know things were as bad as they really were, was because I've tried to learn from the mistakes of my late twenties and early thirties. It was during this time period that I was misdiagnosed and on the wrong medications, but I would flirt with the idea of committing suicide and then voluntarily check myself into the unit. I would sensationalize things, making them all bigger than life. So mixed in with all of the lies and manipulative stories was me using the locked mental health unit as a spa when things got too bad for me to deal with them.

The irony of this is that even with the meds that I'm currently on (as I type this) I don't see myself as psych patient. Other than a few diagnoses that allow the meds to be covered by insurance, I don't really carry any definitive psychiatric label that I'm aware of. About two weeks into the dark period at the end of the session, Doc wrote me a note that said, "You react normally to normal people and normal situations."

I read it, but I didn't "get" it. And I'm rather certain that the reason I didn't get it was because nothing felt normal. On a scale of one to ten, with one being no emotional pain at all, I was living my life at a ten on a daily basis. Ten being I hate myself all the time, I'm angry with myself all the time, I'm a failure, and the world would be better off without me.

The thing is that I'm a Christ follower, which I'll be the first to admit will never make me perfect or actually anything more or less than a person who must daily ask for forgiveness. It does however center me frequently and help me to see that love and compassion and empathy go much farther than any of the alternatives. I love to worship God and feel that He hears my worship best when I am playing my flute. I also believe that God hears me when I pray and that God is a friend of mine.

It wasn't until this morning that I realized that when I turtle from the world, I kind of turtle from God too. You see, instead of talking with God while this was going on, I did a lot more talking to Him. If I were to put the way it felt into words, it was as if I was hiding behind a wall—no—it was closer to me being in a spiritual sensory deprivation tank and shouting into the darkness, hoping God hears me in my anger and frustration and fear but hearing nothing in response but the echo of my own empty words.

It's hard to think of God as a loving father when you are used to being hurt by those whom you love and care about. It's hard to see the truth for what it is. In the movie *Pretty Woman*, there are these two lines that kind of sum it all up. Vivian says, "People put you down enough, and you start to believe it" and "The bad stuff is easier to believe."

As far as I am concerned, that pretty much lays it all right out there. I believe we are conditioned to believe the worst, not just about ourselves but life in general. That's why the five o'clock news leads, with all the bad stuff, despite the fact that there are hundreds of thousands of acts of love, kindness, and compassion that go on every day. We don't look for it, so why bother reporting it? It's so much more lucrative to lead with the scandal, the murder, or the unthinkable crime. So as a result, you are lucky if you get more than one or two "human interest stories" that take any of the good events into consideration during any news broadcast no matter what time it's on.

I'm certain this isn't what God intended of us. I know that the Bible tells me I have value and that God cares so much about me that He made a way for me to be close to Him. Got thinks I'm good stuff (even when I don't)

So the question remains: Who moved last? God is all around me and in me, so it's never a case of God walking away from me. I may turtle and walk away from my friends and, yes, even try to outrun God, but He has never left me not even once. Even if I try to convince myself talking to Him is the same as listening for God's voice, that doesn't make it true.

There is nothing I can do personally to destroy the stigma that is associated with talking about being suicidal. I can tell my story every chance I get trying to make it easier for the next person who comes along, but until people start to look for opportunities to talk about having the desire to commit suicide, it will remain taboo.

As for me, I have a great deal of work left to do. By the way, I have pulled out of the dark and twisted fog and up into the light. I don't know how to tell the difference between when I need to ask for help and when I'm okay. I don't know how to be in the dark, twisted, and broken place and be around people. And I still need to find a way to not be afraid to ask for help when I need it.

The thing is God's got me, and I know that He is not going anywhere. So it turns out the appropriate question is not so much who moved last as it is which direction am I moving in, and even then the question has more to do with faith and forgiveness (of myself) than it does with crossing the borderline.

28

The Last Time Was the Last Time, Right?

I know so much more now than when I started this journey of realizing who I am, and as it turns out, this journey has also taught me who I am not. Now every time I hit one of these dark patches where things get all twisted up, it doesn't matter if it's just a little rough patch or if I end up sitting in my car, trying to figure out if there is a viable exit strategy for me to jump off the planet. Every single time, right now, I think this will be the last time. I know that every time before this, God has brought me through, and now I know the truth. I choose to believe that this will not happen again.

Yet right now, having just come out of this four weeks of darkness, I'm left trying to figure out where it all went wrong. I used to believe that all of it was only my fault. The thing is, this time there were two specific life events. The first triggered me to get to that dark place where I totally loathed myself and have no belief in who I was and, frankly, shook up my entire belief system. The second (falsely) confirmed that hatred that I had for myself and told me that I was exactly where I deserved to be in life.

I could rehash the specifics of the events, but if you are reading this, there is probably a reason for it. You may have been through a part of a borderline personality disorder diagnosis (as a patient, friend, family, or caregiver) or have a history of mental or emotional illness, dysfunction or some level of abuse. If so, you will understand what I mean when I tell you it's so hard not to read between the lines when a person in a traditional authority role in your life is berating you and telling you that you are less than you are even when that's not what the same word would sound like to someone who doesn't know your history.

Then things get even worse if you've spent your life trying to jump on landmines before they explode. You draw the lines that you hear even if words aren't directly spoken. In the latter incident, I actually said, "I'm a horrible person." And the person with whom I was having the conversation said, "I never said that." My response: "You didn't have to."

If you talked to this person (without me around and them knowing that I would have no knowledge of the conversation) you would be told that there was nothing but support there.

I candidly believe that is what she totally believes. Here's the thing. Once you are a participant in an abusive cycle on either end (willing or unwilling), it gets easier to accept each time it happens to continue to participate in the cycle of abuse and manipulations.

Here are the most basic of truths that apply to all human beings no matter what they've done.

1. God made me!
2. God loves me!
3. God says I have value and deserve to be loved!
4. Anything that anyone says to me does not change any part of points 1, 2, and 3!

So how do I get from here to trying to figure out how to off myself and destroy one of God's creations? How do I get to believing that the world would be better off without me and that if any part of what someone else says it true, then all the work I've been doing for the past ten years means nothing?

I wish I could sit here and tell you I have a good answer. I guess in some ways I do, but the thing is I keep shifting all the blame back to me along with the responsibilities. If my faith were stronger, I know that would help. But I know how strong God is, so why do I keep thinking I have to be the one to fix things? If I would just keep myself taking with God, it would keep me from believing the lies that I have learned as "truth" over the better part of the last forty years.

The thing is when you're there, when you are sitting in your own skin and all you can think is that the world would be a better place without you, it's all lies, but it all sounds like the truth. If I ever heard another person talking to someone the way that I talk to myself when I get into the most dark and twisted places, I would be absolutely outraged.

It angers me to hear people bashing other people. You've seen it here when I talk about racism or not being accepting of other people for who they are. You may have even read the part of the Bible where God said that we are to love others as we love our self. So here is another piece of this puzzle put in front of me by my therapist. When I don't love me, I am disobeying God. I know this. I've gotten this for the better part of two years now and still it happens.

It all comes back to one question: Do I honestly believe that I am a person who is worthy of love respect peace and prosperity (God's plan for those who trust Him)?

I'm scared; I admit it. I know my God is big, but I also know that I am small. And I mess up; in my opinion, that happens a great deal. I am, however, slightly aware that it may happen less frequently than it feels like it does.

Last session, Doc asked me what my easiest sin was. It took me forever to figure it out because it happens so frequently that I don't even think of it, which seems kind of off since anger is one of the seven deadly sins. You know that one thing that is my kryptonite? It's believing the lies and not loving myself like I should. That's enough to keep me from trusting God like I should and could be enough to throw my back over the borderline any day.

29

Sleep Deprivation

I'm alone on a Saturday night as I write this. There's this point in the process, whatever process I'm in right now. Is it healing, is it detox, or withdrawal from addiction, getting over PTSD or some unrecognizable version of Stockholm syndrome, or just the combo pack? But there is this point in the process where you have to start identifying things like fears, addictions, coping, and defense mechanisms that are all issues of your past. If you identify them, then you take that first step, right?

What if it isn't the first step? I can't sleep? I haven't been able to consistently sleep through the night since I don't know when. (Literally can't give you a month since my teens where I could sleep through the night with any consistency.) That's part of what started the entire misdiagnosis thing, which brings me to the fact that all of the meds, even when I was misdiagnosed and in the fog of the medication that was prescribed for me (that I didn't need). I couldn't sleep, and there is no medication that I can be given (short of full sedation) that would make it so.**

Here's the kicker. When I go to West Virginia and sleep in my childhood bedroom at the house my great aunt and uncle now own, I sleep like a baby bear cub!

More than once, Doc has said that we need to take a look at why. So I (brainchild that I am) brought it up as something we should attack last session. You see the thing I do when I have some kind of idea where I would like to start session. It's easy to think that I would try to pre-guess how the session will go. However, the preplanning of conversations (even therapeutic ones) is something I gave up with trying to manipulate people and situations with every move I made.

Another thing you should know is that I am in the habit of sending Doc e-mails about what I would like to go over in therapy because I know me. I know if there is something that is scaring me I may want to talk about it today, but that doesn't mean that I'll be brave enough to bring it up in session. So my sending it when I am strong enough (usually no less than three or four days before session) is my own way of getting it on the agenda without having to be strong enough in the moment to say, "Hey, we need to work on (insert issue here)."

It's when I'm sitting there in session, and we're going through the list from my e-mail that I realize that any one particular discussion isn't going to end well. That I, in fact, haven't thought it through. Today in session, Doc gets to the third point of a four-point e-mail. The sleep thing.

He asks me what bad things have happened to me at night. I sit there trying to remember. Trying to go back and—I really don't know if I've mentioned it here before but I don't remember a lot of my life, not even the stuff you are supposed to remember (graduations, birthdays) let alone life's little events.

I kind of know when things happened. I mean I have the major marker dates, and I do my best to remember when things get inserted between these major mile markers. I can remember a lot more of the last few years, basically since I've started this round of therapy.

So asking me if there were bad things that happened at night was literally like trying to make me remember words that were supposed to fill up a blank page long after they have been erased. I've gotten some memories back. It comes in bits and pieces and, sometimes, really strange things. Like tonight, I randomly remember a fact about sock monkeys. My Grammie used to keep them on the stairs that led up to her bedroom. I had totally forgotten that face when I used a tie-dye sock monkey as a stress doll for the better part of eighteen months.

So tonight, I type this, feeling like a total failure because I can't sleep. I am also someone who is scared out of her mind. I've met a guy, which may not be as significant as it feels in this moment. I've really not done a lot of dating, trying to be respectful of the relationship that I am going to have, but I am so scared because historically, I'm a failure at this kind of relationship. This man is loving and strong and respectful. So I'm scared that he is going to see me for the mess that I am and head for the hills.

This would be a totally inappropriate thing to bring up in this chapter if it weren't for that fact that the only two bad things I could remember happening at night involved men that I thought I loved deeply. Granted I didn't know what love was then.

Stuff happens—good stuff and bad stuff, sane and crazy stuff—all of it happens in both the night and the day, and you know what? The world keeps turning. It does. The clocks keep ticking weather I sleep or not.

I don't know. I try so hard to be the chick who has it all together who can find her way through, and I can't even remember where I've been. Right now, I know my problem. I can't sleep at least not with any consistency.

It's not twenty-four hours since I wrote the first part of this chapter, which makes it Sunday night. Ironically, or maybe not so much, I went to church and worshiped God and then sat there. Church or (and I thank God for this) the church that I regularly attend is one of my softest places in the world. It's proof to me that after things go wrong, after I've done things wrong, God cares about me enough to put people in my path who speak life into me.

So I'm sitting there in church after the service is over, just trying to remember anything that I've forgotten (in relationship to Doc's question in therapy). I'm wondering if there could be one memory that is the key to finding out why I'm not sleeping with any consistency. You know what?

I could not remember anything in the pew on Sunday that I didn't think of when I was in Doc's office on Friday.

The thing is, over the years, I've tried it all: prayer, meditation, breathing exercises, muscle exercises, routines, hot baths, how showers, warm milk, music, no music, dark rooms, swirling patterns, herbal remedies.

I don't play games like I used to. Okay, I still have a few of those vices left, but really these days, it's more the games that I play with myself.

My point is that I'm sitting there in church after service is over and genuinely trying to remember, and I just don't know how to do it. The more time I spend not remembering things, the angrier I get with myself. So tonight I'm sitting here all medicated and compliant, but right now, I'm also sure there isn't much sleep in my immediate future, which means that I am going to go back to therapy this week and I do—I don't know what.

I just don't have the strength anymore to try to predict what will happen. I told Pastor today, and I know it's true. When you rehearse in your head what you will say and then try to predict what the other person will say, it leads to hiding things it takes a lot of energy and effort. I'm just over that.

I know life is best lived in the moment, with kindness and empathy and passion and compassion. I know when things are hidden, they don't go away, which is definitely ironic because it turns out this chapter is about my past having gone away, or at least this week, I haven't been able to remember it.

I know being honest beats the alternative every single time with absolutely no exceptions.

I know there are more than two sides to every single story.

I know every story has a beginning even if you can't remember it. And …

With all that being said, tonight I know that I am not my biggest fan.

I was told today (in a moment of total self-loathing) that God needs people to hear my story, especially in chapters like this one where my faults and my battle fill the page. I can only pray that is true.

I think a lot of the time I try to do things for the right reasons: to honor God and make it about Him and His love, showing people that I love them hopefully like God loves me; to give; and if I'm so blessed, to lighten the load of others. I think maybe I get that part right more often that I don't. I think it's hard for me to admit that because it's not so often that it feels that way or that I see the good in me.

Tonight, none of that helps me get to sleep and actually neither does writing the rest of this chapter tonight. So I'm going to close the laptop for the night and try to get some sleep and, no matter what the outcome, face the day tomorrow. Therapy doesn't come until the end of the week. Perhaps I'll remember something by then.

**It turns out that while on the correct medication (Remeron), I not only have a more peaceful waking hours but also am finding myself sleeping with much greater consistency.

30

It Hurts the Most When There Is Pain

I'm trying to understand what is going on, but I'm coming up short. Last session, was good but ended in this odd lopsided way which left me hurting on behalf of those who have lost the battle due to self-inflicted demise, which is a very gentle way of saying suicide. Adding to this sad, angry emptiness was the fact that I was given a homework assignment that I totally got the wrong thing out of (which falls under the self-imposed statue of let's tar and feather T. R. for being stupid) and the fact that the following weekend was the anniversary of the last holiday I got to spend with a loved one who is no longer around.

Add to that the fact that the double bind drama was in full swing at home, and I am all too aware that people who are supposed to be important and consistent resources in my life don't like or respect me. You have found my tipping point. It was an extended three-day weekend that was filled with intermittent tears and self-loathing, which was only interrupted by my berating myself for not being a better, stronger person.

The thing is, it starts this downward spiral, and it's like a plane that is spiraling to earth—about to spin in—that can't be pulled up. First I start by mentally berating myself. Ironically as this is starting up, I get an e-mail notification that my pharmacy rewards card program now has a special where I can get in store credit for the exact type of razor blade I have used for years to cut myself.

So now added to the fact that I am in this horrible self-talk dialogue is the fact that everything in me wants to cut my skin and peel myself like a grape. Right now, I just want to go find a place where I wouldn't be found for a few months and just end it all. I know that sounded harsh, but it's rather accurate.

So what do I do? I have several option available, good options. Options that could change the outcome of my day, weekend, and quite possibly my whole life. I have good friends and family who are positive influences in my life, and if I asked for help, they would be there.

Yet somehow, that's not where I go. I keep the self-talk going and then put on a playlist of songs that I listen to when things seem bad, and I'm okay with everything feeling that way.

I go back to my life and continue to work around the house and life and go to church and do "the therapy thing," and today it's all just proving to myself what a loser I am.

On this day in particular, I begin reading web articles on brilliantly talented people who have committed suicide, then I begin watching some select episodes of a few different shows that show examples of emotionally distressed persons who either do or don't survive their distress.

The thing I can't seem to understand is why I go this route; it's the mental and emotional gymnastic equivalent of falling off a motorcycle and getting bad road rash and rubbing the wound with salt then pouring rubbing alcohol into the wound—the exception being that this feels like it could kill me.

I'm so tired of everyone telling me how good of a person I am and how strong I am, how I am a fighter. It doesn't feel like I'm a fighter at all. Actually today, I have nothing left to give.

31

Alone in the Desert

I don't think we've talked about what happens when everything calms down, when thoughts come one at a time instead of six or eight deep, and the thought you have isn't racing ten thousand miles a minute and colliding with another thought, throwing you off track. Suddenly you are not filled with self-hatred every minute of every day. What happens when it literally feels like the pressure around your physical being is less, and because of the lack of psychological pain, you feel like you can breathe again.

For me, this equals an emptiness that I didn't know to anticipate. I was expecting relief but I didn't realize how dependent I was on the hatred of myself and the emotions or thoughts that surround that. I didn't know that it kept me going and propelled me forward. The fact that I needed to keep everything inside in order and stop the unforeseen from happening was intense. So now there is this loneliness.

You know how I like to put feelings into words. It's like dropping a penny into a very deep dark well. The anticipation of that penny hitting the water can be intense. Since it's a deep well and you can't see to the bottom, you may lean over and turn your head and wait for the splash. Then when that splash is gone, there is just that deep hallow empty silence, and you know nothing comes next. It's like that—almost exactly!

I find myself wanting to write that it is anticlimactic, but it's closer to a full reversal or path change. You see, I've been carrying all this for longer than I care to actually admit; I think it has been at least twenty-seven years of anger, frustration, and the endless thoughts of self-loathing, hatred, and desire for extinction. I've been trying to defend myself when I should have been just living life.

So tonight I am dealing with two things:

1. Why didn't someone tell me about this sooner?
   - I don't like the answer to this one because a lot of the responsibility for this is laid at my own feet. I was afraid for decades to express the feelings and thoughts I was having because they made me feel like some kind of monster or freak. When I was growing up, there wasn't much talking about feelings going on, and from that, I extrapolated that it shouldn't be done. I came to this conclusion all on my own. You see, the people you are counting on to help you (therapists, doctors, friends, clergy) can't see what is hidden. So if you don't let them know there is a problem, the obvious thought is that everything is okay. On the other hand, you can't let them know there is a problem if you don't realize that life isn't supposed to be like this.

Yet somehow, it seems like someone should have heard the cry I never made. There was no way until I felt comfortable enough with who I am (or so afraid that who I am wouldn't actually exist anymore) that I would have reached out and said, "I'm scared"—like I did that day when I called my therapist to ask for help and ended up having the right medication prescribed for the first time in my life. I have to think that had something to do with the fact that for the first time I was totally honest and open about what I needed and where I was.

2. How do I deal with the loneliness?
   - I said earlier that I didn't know this was coming, and in the interest of full disclosure, I'm not sure which

would have been worse. I guess it kind of feels like losing an imaginary friend in a way. I don't know there may be some version of PTSD or Stockholm syndrome that comes into play here. Maybe not but the thing is that everything is different. I've never been one to have memories really. It's always been knowing not remembering the events that mark time. If I'm lucky, I might be able to tell you when something happened between the mile markers. Now I'm getting back pieces of things in small amounts. It's only a few things, but they feel like actual memories, which really just feels odd. It's almost like I'm experiencing short clips of my life back one movie at a time—more like a short—then I'm left dealing with all this stuff that I haven't had to handle before. They don't tell you when you are trying to get all healed and complete again that you will feel lonelier than you have ever been, and I know why. No one would sign up for that because it hurts deeper than it did just to lose someone and try to put your life back together again.

I never wanted this, but something tells me it's leading me to the place that I want to go. There is this road in Pennsylvania that I had the pleasure of "cruising" last fall. It's in the woods, and its curviness and forestation reminded me a lot of West Virginia. Driving through this area is amazingly beautiful. It's a local recreation road—not on the regular tourist map or anything—and the road is kind of more filled with potholes than filled with road. And the potholes are deep.

All that being said, there are two places in the road. If you make it through the potholes where the road goes through the creek—not over it, but through it. There is cement road that is literally covered by water deep enough to open the doors and dip your feet in the stream of water that is crossing the road. It's peaceful and serene, but you can't get to it without getting past the potholes.

It's not a road that I would ever take my little car down. That road would tear my car up, but if I was equipped with the right vehicle (one with four-wheel drive), I would probably hit it at least once a month or so until the frigid weather sets in.

So life is like this road in the woods—filled with potholes, beautiful but in places dark and perhaps scary with spiders, bugs, and snakes. It may not be the most glamorous of similes but rather accurate. I don't want to go back to being dishonest and hiding my feelings, and I'm definitely anxious about moving forward. It's lonely because it feels like no one understands and because I can't seem to find the right words tonight to express how lonely it is.

The hardest part of all of this for me is that I don't know what to do when the loneliness envelops me. I was prepared for things to get better, but it turns out I didn't know what it would feel like when things changed. It also turns out that the status quo—no matter how good or bad it is—can feel safe and secure and predictable.

For me, the status quo normally involved the day ending and me making lists of how I have failed or trying to find ways to avoid failing tomorrow. It also involved me beating myself up verbally and emotionally (at times, physically) and then—if I'm lucky—falling asleep, more normally not falling asleep to such thoughts.

In my life I've been far crueler to me than to anyone else, and I never realized how much I depended on that to get me through.

I finished writing this chapter a month ago. I came back and read it today and realized that I missed on major component:

The component of the good-intentioned bystander. This time through the psychotherapeutic dance, I've been so blessed by God to have these amazing people in my life. Most folks would call them friends, but the reality is that they are in some ways as close as family. I don't always see them all as often as I should. The thing is, they know how lonely things are right now, and more have told me this in my deepest pit of loneliness when the self-doubt and self-loathing subside: "You are not alone."

The thing is that they can be standing right in front of me, in the very same room and make that statement. In that exact moment, stand-

ing there with them, I couldn't be more alone if I were in the padded room of the locked unit.

There is still a piece of me that isolates myself. That says I'm too broken to be fixed and the damages done by the stuff that I'm dealing with isn't important enough to bother someone else with.

Yet somehow, I've realize in the last couple of days that this is the stuff that decisions to end life are made over. It's crazy that there is so much stigma associated with this. That is the reason why there are so many people out there who are ashamed to discuss it. That's why I was too ashamed to admit to it.

I was ashamed because I felt this way. In the end, it led me to the locked adult psychiatric unit. This led me to become ashamed because I didn't think I was as "disadvantaged" as some of the others were or like they were "so much" different than I was. Even now as I have all these amazing people frequently surrounding me, I'm too scared to reach out for help.

It isn't possible that I am scared of what they think. I wouldn't be sitting here writing this if that were my main concern. Or would I? Or am I?

32

One Favorite Thing

It probably won't come as much of a surprise to you that one of my "favorite" (because I've already mentioned it) things to do when I'm in the land of the dark and twisted emotional place is look at some of my favorite episodes of television shows or movies that deal with someone who is in a bad emotional or mental space too (i.e., in the locked adult unit). There is something soothing about watching those who fictionally either succumb to or defy and conquer the demons within, which as far as I am concerned, can so easily infiltrate my thoughts. It doesn't really matter to me what "brand" of demon it is. It can be schizophrenia, bipolar, traumatic amnesia, addiction, delusion, and the list goes on and on. I must admit that I do have a few favorites to watch, and that's part of the reason that I subscribe to subscription video services.

What I didn't realize until this week is that I've been learning amazing lessons from these episodes. Some of which I may have literally watched at least a hundred times or more. So I was sitting in my therapy session on Friday and Doc was talking about, or more specifically trying to get me to talk about, a topic. I see where he was going but not where he was trying to get me to. I had something that I wanted to discuss that, in my opinion, was far higher on the priority scale. So out of the blue and without any real reason, I said something like this: "I need to change topics. If you want to keep talking about this, we can, but I'm really feeling the need to deflect and run down another trail. It's your call, but

I'm trying to not just deflect or shut down here. Do you want me to stay on this subject?"

Doc just looked at me as if I had some kind of major revelation. It was that look (followed by dialogue) that confirmed he knew that my deflections and snarky comments were designed to get things diverted to whatever it was that I wanted to talk about.

After his comment about my asking permission, I threw back that it was something that I learned from the television episodes referencing two in particular.

This process is much harder than it looks on television, especially on days like yesterday morning when you've moved up your therapy appointment so that you have one less day to jump ship or, in total candor the planet, to sit there and talk about everything. All the dark and twisted thoughts and the hatred you have for yourself, the love you have for the people who have harmed you over and over again, not to mention the desire to save them despite the fact that they have pushed you back into the fire over and over again.

It's easy for me to take the quick and snarky and defensive retort instead of holding my own feet to the fire and playing the cards that have been dealt in any given moment of the therapy session or for that matter in life. I think most of the people who know me really well would tell you that I am generally kind, gentle, sharp-witted and always willing to help where I can.

I try to be giving and not ask for much in return, and most of the time, that includes me not asking for help even if I need it. The sweet irony is that I now have this amazing team of friends that God has surrounded me with. The honest truth is that God loves me and so do these friends no matter what. But they have the good and godly sense to tell me when I've overstepped or am headed the wrong direction. I have this one friend who, several times a week, sends me these amazing notes of encouragement and godly counsel.

The thing is that no matter how uplifting or encouraging these messages are in the moments when I'm in the darkest corners of emotions, as soon as I've gotten the message, I have the feeling that I have let her down even before I finish reading the messages.

She and I have spoken about this on more than one occasion. What she doesn't know is that in a few days or a week or whenever it is that the dark cloud passes, I reread them, and they are some of the most treasured gifts that I have. Even when I am at my darkest, she sees the person that God thinks and relying on what I feel.

The deflection thing—it was learned but not off of any of the TV shows or movies that I've watched. I learned that in the life, and it's probably saved my life but not as many times as I've regretted it; although frequently, it's rather harmless.

The thing is, by talking it out as I'm able and actually paying attention to others and identifying with them, I can learn more about how and why I behave like I do. Then I get to do things like ask for permission (during a talk therapy session) to deflect and run down my own therapeutic rabbit trail. Instead of just ping and ricochet—it's the adult way to do therapy. Admitting to what's going on instead of trying to play games because those times when I don't ask for permission, Doc knows what's going on.

33

Everything Looks So Much Easier from the Outside

Well it does, even the tricky stuff. That's what the saying "The grass is always greener" is all about. Frequently I find myself wondering, if not saying, "I could do that, couldn't I?" or "I wish I could do that." Why? It looks or seems simple. Let me tell you there is nothing simple about being diagnosed with mental illness or being labeled as an emotionally distressed person.

It's not like having a heart attack or cancer or, for that matter, irritable bowel syndrome (yep I went there), but mental and emotional health is something that needs to be dealt with just as seriously. It's just as much of a disease. The only thing is that the stigma attached to it makes it something that you are embarrassed to talk about. The kicker is that only by talking about is the first step in starting to get better.

For me, in addition to being ashamed of the diagnosis, even after the wrong diagnosis was shed and I was left with the one correct diagnosis, I would run into people who refused to believe the diagnosis is true. Having been diagnosed with borderline personality disorder, the number one comment I would get is that there is nothing wrong with your personality. My personality frankly had little to do with me being diagnosed. The irony, for me, is that the med doc and the therapist who diagnosed and treated me initially misdiagnosed half of it and hit the bull's eye right in the center with the borderline diagnosis.

I used to hear the following responses all the time when someone said that I was on medication or a psych patient:

- *Oh, that can't be true.*
- *But she's such a nice gal.*
- *She has such a sharp mind*
- *There's no way that can be true. She's just trying to get attention.*

Others will pretend to not even hear the subject matter, and that is just when they find out you are in therapy or a psych patient. Then if you need to take meds for it, the comments are worse. And if the meds have side effects, there is an entirely different set of well-intentioned comments designed to keep you from actually having to talk about or acknowledge the topic.

One of the tricky things is that most psych meds take time to kick in and work. They usually need to be adjusted and re-adjusted. The people who live with these challenges fight battles every single day and frequently deal with fears that are beyond what most can imagine. Things like the following:

- *Will my medication work today?*
- *Will my medication stop working today?*
- *What happens if it all falls apart?*
- *What if it all starts to work and come together, how do I keep the wheels from falling off of that wagon? (My biggest fear when I was counting on the meds alone)*

To be candid, I don't know when my issues started. I literally can't remember a time when I wasn't exhibiting some form of low self-esteem issues, and I know I started to show the first symptoms of what turned out to be borderline personality disorder long before I turned sixteen.

No one talks about it or at least didn't in the places I was from. It's something that just happened to me over time. The thoughts begin to race, or the fear is paralyzing. And you just can't move forward (sometimes literally and sometimes figuratively). I would hear the voices and dream the dreams and, at times, couldn't tell where reality started or stopped.

If you are blessed enough to get a good med doc or therapist—and you need it—you will eventually find your way to medication. Would you like to know where the rub lies for the psych patient on medication? First you have to talk yourself into taking med, and if you're at the point where you know you need your life to change, you'll take the medicine. Then when you take the medicine, it helps a little. Ten the med doc tweaks it, then things start getting better. You have good days—strike that—great days. You put in a full week of work, and you don't want to harm yourself for a day or a week. You sit down to read a book and can actually make it through an entire chapter, or you watch a whole movie from beginning to end without getting distracted. Then it happens. You wonder if you really need the medication at all.

For me, it never mattered how often I went on and off the medication; when it was working I was really convinced I didn't need it.

The thing patients and family members of patients need to know is that the more you go on and off these medications, the more your body builds up a tolerance to them and the less likely they are to be as effective the next time you go back on the med. It's literally a fight for your life every time you go.

For me, the meds I used to be on (when I was on the wrong medication) came with a long list of side effects.

- *Weight gain*
- *Muscle twitches*
- *Lactation*
- *Short term memory loss*
- *The inability to keep pace with reality*
- *Feeling like I was living life in slow motion*

The list of side effects is much longer than that, but the entire time I was taking them, I was hearing the following:

"You're fine."
"It's all in your head."
"You need to give it to God."

The medication—it put me in a fog. It was like thinking and walking and living through this cloud of marshmallows. Everything felt like it was in slow motion, and because of that, even on the best of days, I was defeated. I didn't understand or, more correctly, didn't know that I could understand what was going on. That was what life for me used to be like on the wrong medications.

34

The Cut Is Shallow, but the Pain Runs Deep

So when I was cutting, that makes it sound like it was only once or twice or for a defined period of time, which isn't the case at all. It's something that came and went. It's something that, for well over a decade, I thought of at least every day—usually more than once. Now it's something that comes back to me as something I used to do and in a very over-romanticized way, something that gave me great comfort and release from the guilt of the sigma of mental health issues.

If you look at my scars today, it's crazy to think that it was me who did that. With that being said, it's still a desire that comes up from time to time. I have to be candid. I believe that it's a sin and that my body is a temple. However, that doesn't mean that from time to time I'm not tempted.

The thing is that the cutting only took away (or maybe mitigated is a better word) the hurt that was going on in my head and all around me. Mine was very ritualistic and very—from what I understand, usually for people, it tends to be more of an impulsive thing. Mine was calculated. Planned out. My razor blades were sterilized; my bandages and antiseptic were laid out on a towel.

I keep trying to figure out to how explain the why and the how of it to someone who hasn't lived through it, and I can't. It made things better, but then hours later, I would feel like a freak or a monster—or I should say more of a freak and monster because that was how I felt about myself on any given day.

I've been blessed to have the courage of my conviction that this is something that people hide and that I don't want someone to have to be ashamed or embarrassed like I was because they need help. So I'm typing this to you know and have told my story to friends and family members and even strangers who are cutting or know someone who cuts. It's not something that you should have to hide or be afraid to mention.

For me, it was all a part of the pain being so, so bad that I needed to find a way to express it and get through it. So I sliced my arm with a blade—usually my upper right bicep because it was easiest to hide under a sleeve.

It never was a permanent resolution to anything. If you look at my arm now, it's a map of scars which for me serve as a reminder that God heals, and there is mercy and grace. If I can do it, I know you can cross whatever borderline is in front of you!

35

Measuring Up

Today I caught it happening. I didn't realize it was actually taking place. I went to dial the phone and found my brain saying, "Wait a minute, this person you want to dial is probably too busy with other things to take your call."

It started me thinking, and you know what? I couldn't tell you how many times in a week I do just that—think of myself as less important than those around me. My friends and family and even acquaintances for most of my life—I have (without realizing it) put them all up on a pedestal and thought that their time was much more valuable than mine.

I know I've touched on this in a few chapters of this book, but it is something that I need to emphasize before this book ends. Every life is important! Everyone influences other people. We, as individuals, seem to put this class system into place and everyone's relationship in its own hierarchy of people who we will or won't bother with different stuff, depending on where we prioritize the topic. Here are some of the values that my structure revolves around.

- Job (including homemaker and stay-at-home mom—or whatever label you want to put on it. Are you kidding me? These people raise children and families for a living)
- Do they have a husband/wife and or kids?
- Community involvement

That's just the start of the list. I'm not the gal who tends put priority or greater-lesser value on physical things or skin color when it comes to assigning importance to people. I know that every person who walks this earth—no matter what choices they have made or what they have done or not done—is a creation of the God who made the universe and some of God's best work.

What I don't know how to do is not minimize my own value or that of my effectiveness in interactions with people.

The hard thing for me to face up to is the fact this is something that I have to work on myself. It's not one of the issues that a therapist could help me with. It's one of those things I have to figure out on my own. I need to start finding ways to stop devaluing myself.

So it turns out that the question I find myself asking today is what am I measuring up to? If I keep trying to measure myself by the yardstick of success of others, it won't work. I have to take things one step at a time and start measuring my life by that yardsticks that matter. One of the biggest factors is am I respectful and loving and kind to everyone I meet. If the answer is anything less than yes, I'm not measuring up.

36

I'm Not So Different After All

It's the trickery of the world. Most of us want to be "normal," and in the same breath, we want to believe that we move to the beat of our own drum. This is, for me, one of the hard parts of crossing the borderline. The "wanting to be just like everyone else" thing I get, but part of dealing with the fact that I have crossed that line and not wanting to go back over it changes who I am.

My book is just one way that I talk all about how I dealt with the process, but in order for it to stick and really count myself as better, I have to realize that I am no longer the person with borderline personality disorder. I need to know that it's okay to be "normal" and not carry a diagnosis. Even with that being said, what is normal for me may not be normal for the world.

It's a hard thing to embrace when you have identified yourself for so long as—it's not Munchausen (you know, that thing where you fake symptoms to get attention). It's not that at all. Personally, I spent so much time working things out, keeping my guard up and making statements like "I'm borderline." My mental health diagnoses, at least in my mind, defined who I was. At times, they dictated how I behaved even when they weren't really affecting me and for some time, after I no longer carried the diagnosis because I simply believed it was still true.

There is a difference. There was a long stretch of time when I thought, more than anything, I wanted to be "normal" like the others around me, and at the same time, I felt like a ticking time bomb.

I also felt like I was responsible for those around me and minimizing damage in my wake. If I take my arms and let them hang by my side and then lift my arms outward so they are parallel with my shoulders, that space in between my fingertips—it turns out that's the only space that I can actually control.

People get hurt all the time. People leave or die, and abandonment happens. That's not quite as scary now as it used to be. Lately, on more than one occasion, I have found myself having to walk away from relationships to protect myself. It used to be that I couldn't handle that.

It turns out that being your own advocate—kindly, respectfully, and ferociously—is a big part of being "normal." So if you are looking to be normal, just live a life with integrity and passion, love God, and show that same love to people. That's what normal should be like. It's really not so much about me and how I'm turning out.

Epilogue
Moving Forward!

I've spent my entire life feeling like I wasn't good enough, or at least I don't remember a time when I felt I was strong enough to take my next breath. Something amazing happened this morning.

I was doing that this morning when suddenly, it occurred to me that I haven't even thought about cutting in the last two weeks. Not I haven't done it, not I've fought the urge, but it hasn't even occurred to me that it was an option. Even bigger than that, for the first time in my life, I feel like I can do life and that it's almost possible that I can succeed. Actually, it feels totally possible that I can succeed, that I can write this book and the next one. (Yes, I know what the title is but you'll have to wait it out.). I can make all these big changes that I am looking to make—professionally, personally and emotionally.

I'm an asthmatic, and literally this is what it feels like when you take that first deep breath after you have not been able to breath. It's like getting my life back. I say back, but it's like I've got a shot for the very first time.

No matter what is ahead of me, I know that all feelings are only temporary. What I know now (that I didn't know when I started writing this book) is that life, for me, even after the talk therapy is over, will continue to be a process of meds, talking/journaling/writing, following God, and staying very involved in church. I know that what I am meant to do with my life is to help others who are having mental and emotional issues learn how to deal with life.

So this is it. The end of this page and with that the end of the book. The stuff that got me to the point of writing it—if I had to do it over again, I would change a lot if I could. In the same breath, I could not have shared this with you if it hadn't happened. You see, I've always had a group of people telling me I could do things my entire life, but it was always laced with their own agenda. Even therapists that I have been to in the past have tried to get me to the point where they wanted me to be.

The thing is, the therapist that I was seeing as I was writing the majority of this book allowed me to be myself during the process. I have to tell you I wasn't prepared for that. I was called out on the stuff that I was doing even when I didn't realize it was going on. One such day, he asked me a question, and I couldn't come up with an answer or at least one I thought he would want to hear. As a result, there were twenty minutes of silence. We were both playing the same card, that one card in the deck which says *he who speaks first loses*. The thing was, I wanted to be the one to lose that day, but I didn't know how. Finally, I bit the bullet and budged and said I don't know what you want me to say here, so I don't know how to answer. Then the conversation began about how I was to try to stop trying to guess how the conversations were to go and start saying what I mean.

It was the beginning of the end of that three-second delay I spoke of earlier in this book. It was the beginning of me being able to speak my mind in the moment and not have an agenda and not having to filter my feelings and my emotions. It was a moment that I knew I wouldn't forget, but I never dreamed that I would feel the way I feel today.

The thing with crossing the borderline is that the line keeps moving and gets to be closer on some days and farther behind you on others. It could be something that I struggle against for my entire life, but what I see today for the very first time that I haven't seen before is that it totally could be something that is just behind me. That borderline could just be an obstacle that I have not only crossed but crossed off.

As I sign off and get ready to write the second book, I have two things to say. I can't change the past, but I hope that this can impact the future for a lot of people. Most of all, I'd like to quote my best friend's husband because he and his family have totally impacted my life for the better, so if you hear me say anything, please know Jesus loves you; He really does!

Because what you do with your future and knowing Jesus loves you is the only way you will ever cross the borderline!

About the Author

T. R. Lilly was correctly diagnosed with borderline personality disorder and depression and was misdiagnosed with bipolar disorder. After having been improperly medicated for a condition she didn't have and having multiple admissions to locked psych units, T. R. chose to become her own advocate. She believes that good mental and emotional health can involve any combination of up to three components—talk therapy, medication, and a spiritual connection to God.

T. R. chooses to tell her story at every opportunity to raise awareness for mental health and suicide awareness and is now pursuing an education in the field of psychology and human services. She has spoken out in the community, at work, and in her church.

Her goal is to help all people realize that they have worth, great value and that God loves them. T. R. shares a deep seeded awareness of that pains that come from needing to have better mental and emotional health and is a strong advocate for speaking of these things.

These are the reasons T. R. is passionate in her advocacy of mental health and suicide awareness and sees a need to talk about the things that most people choose to hide.